FINGAL COUNTY LIBRARIES

NF

'08 FCL00000123419

920 KETTLE

Thomas Kettle

✶

WITHDRAWN FROM FINGAL
COUNTY LIBRARY STOCK

D1476437

HISTORICAL ASSOCIATION OF IRELAND

LIFE AND TIMES

NEW SERIES

General Editor: Ciaran Brady

Now available
Thomas Kettle by Senia Pašeta
John Mitchel by James Quinn
Denis Guiney by Peter Costello

Titles are in preparation on Arthur Guinness,
John Charles McQuaid and Isaac Butt

Thomas Kettle

SENIA PAŠETA

✦

Published on behalf of the
Historical Association of Ireland
by

UNIVERSITY COLLEGE DUBLIN PRESS
PREAS CHOLÁISTE OLLSCOILE
BHAILE ÁTHA CLIATH

2008

First published 2008 on behalf of the
Historical Association of Ireland
by University College Dublin Press

© Senia Pašeta, 2008

ISBN 978 –1–906–359–13–3
ISSN 2009–1397

University College Dublin Press
Newman House, 86 St Stephen's Green
Dublin 2, Ireland
www.ucdpress.ie

All rights reserved. No part of this publication
may be reproduced, stored in a retrieval system,
or transmitted in any form or by any means, electronic,
photocopying, recording or otherwise without
the prior permission of the publisher.

CIP data available from the British Library

*The right of Senia Pašeta to be identified as
the author of this work has been asserted by her*

Typeset in Bantry, Ireland in Ehrhardt by Elaine Burberry
Text design by Lyn Davies
Printed in England on acid-free paper by
MPG Books, Bodmin, Cornwall

CONTENTS

ABBREVIATIONS

GAA	Gaelic Athletic Association
IAOS	Irish Agricultural Organisation Society
IPP	Irish Parliamentary Party
IRB	Irish Republican Brotherhood
IWFL	Irish Women's Franchise League
L&H	Literary and Historical Society
NLI	National Library of Ireland
TMKP	T. M. Kettle Papers
UCD	University College Dublin
UIL	United Irish League
UVF	Ulster Volunteer Force
WSPU	Women's Social and Political Union
YIB	Young Ireland Branch of the United Irish League

ACKNOWLEDGEMENTS

I have accumulated a great many debts while writing this book and I wish to thank all the people who provided information and assistance of various kinds. Patrick Maume and Ben Novick generously shared ideas and references, Desmond Murphy and Pauric Dempsey supplied important information and Sean Johnson and Noelle Moran dealt patiently with my drafts. Barbara Mennell has been a dream editor: without her this book would not have seen the light of day. A number of librarians and archivists at UCD helped enormously: I am especially grateful to Eugene Roche from Special Collections, and Séamus Helferty and his colleagues at the Archives Department. Kevin Myers shared conversations and a remarkable collection of letters which deepened my knowledge of Kettle's painful last years, and Esther Murnane allowed me to consult them: their interest and assistance were invaluable. Many friends and colleagues offered constructive criticism and sat patiently through endless – and no doubt tiresome – conversations about Kettle and his place in Irish history. I am particularly grateful to Charles Townshend for reading and commenting on an earlier draft, and to Marc Mulholland, Adrian Gregory and Katarina Pašeta for their interest in and enthusiasm for this biography. It is a great pleasure to be able to acknowledge here the help I received from Roy Foster, both with this book and with many other projects over the years: this is dedicated to him with affection and gratitude.

Finally, heartfelt thanks to Simon Riley who read and corrected drafts, listed to my often disjointed ideas about Kettle, and even visited Kettle sites with me: he and our own little Tom have been delightful companions over the course of this project.

SP
Oxford, 2008

FOREWORD

Originally conceived over a decade ago to place the lives of leading figures in Irish history against the background of new research on the problems and conditions of their times and modern assessments of their historical significance, the Historical Association of Ireland Life and Times series enjoyed remarkable popularity and success. A second series has now been planned in association with UCD Press in a new format and with fuller scholarly apparatus. Encouraged by the reception given to the earlier series, the volumes in the new series will be expressly designed to be of particular help to students preparing for the Leaving Certificate, for GCE Advanced Level and for undergraduate history courses as well as appealing to the happily insatiable appetite for new views of Irish history among the general public.

Ciaran Brady
Historical Association of Ireland

CHRONOLOGY OF KETTLE'S LIFE AND TIMES

1880
Thomas Michael Kettle born on 9 February at Artane, County Dublin.

1883
University College Dublin reorganised under the rectorship of Fr William Delany.

1890–1
Parnell split: the Kettle family remain loyal supporters.

1893
Introduction of the Second Home Rule Bill.

1894
Sent as a boarder to the Jesuit Clongowes Wood College at Sallins, County Kildare; wins prizes and medals for his performance in Intermediate examinations.

1897
Begins at University College Dublin.

1898
Kettle elected auditor of the 'L&H'.

1900
Irish Parliamentary Party reunites.

1901
St Stephen's launched at UCD. Kettle becomes editor in 1903.

1902
Takes a BA in mental and moral science; enters the King's Inns as a law student.

1904
Formation of the Young Ireland Branch of the United Irish League (YIB); Kettle elected president.
Griffith publishes *The Resurrection of Hungary*.

1905
Nationist launched: runs for six months.

1906
Kettle called to the Bar.
Liberal landslide in the general election; Kettle enters parliament as the MP for East Tyrone.

1907
Irish Party rejects the Irish Council Bill.

1908
Irish Universities Act.

1909
Marries Mary Sheehy.

1910
January–February: general election in the United Kingdom: Kettle re-contests and holds his East Tyrone seat; resigns from parliament.
The Day's Burden and *Why Bully Women?* published.

1912
Introduction of the Third Home Rule Bill; publication of *The Open Secret of Ireland*.

1913

Dublin Lock-Out; formation of the Irish Volunteers; formation of the UVF.

1914

Howth gun-running.

Kettle travels to Belgium to buy guns for the Volunteers and witnesses the outbreak of the Great War.

Britain declares war against Germany

Home Rule Act suspended

Redmond commits Irish support to the British war effort; Kettle enlists and is appointed a recruiting agent.

1916

9 September Kettle killed in action.

Introduction

Thomas Michael Kettle was born into politics, and political controversy dominated most of his short life. His boyhood and final years were lived against the backdrop of Irish politics at their most dramatic and demanding – the years between Parnell and Pearse – which witnessed the height of Irish constitutional nationalism and the beginning of its subsequent slide into political irrelevance. He was associated with almost every major political and cultural development that arose during the years 1880–1916, sometimes as a supporter, often as an acerbic critic. A constitutional nationalist to the core, he was nevertheless more aware than most of his contemporaries of the possibilities offered by the extra-parliamentary organisations and mentalities which began to challenge the hegemony of the Irish Party at the turn of the twentieth century. And, unlike most of his less imaginative IPP colleagues, he understood that such challenges must be faced down by a dynamic and modernising party if it hoped to both retain the allegiance of its existing Irish electorate and secure the loyalty of young voters.

Kettle was widely recognised by his contemporaries – admirers and enemies alike – as one of the most outstanding minds of his generation. The contrast between the impact he made on his own contemporaries and his virtual absence from history books for most of the twentieth century is significant, but hardly unique. As his friend William Dawson lamented: 'the violent changes which, since 1916, have swept over Irish politics have well-nigh obliterated all traces of men even more prominent than Tom Kettle, and his memory has, therefore, like that of many, suffered an undeserved eclipse'.[1] He experienced the same fate at the hands of post-1916 propagandists and historians as many of his constitutional nationalist colleagues. But since he was not as prominent as men like John Redmond or John Dillon in the twilight years of parliamentary politics, he failed even to achieve a level of notoriety that might have ensured he would be remembered even in the most negative of terms. Additionally, Kettle committed a number of other offences which virtually guaranteed that his reputation would not survive the doctrinaire political and intellectual climate which cast its shadow over independent Ireland: he warned against the wholesale gaelicisation of Ireland, he actively advocated Home Rule within the Empire and, perhaps most damaging of all, he supported passionately – though not uncritically – the participation of Irish troops in the Great War. These convictions were intimately related and formed part of a wider ideological position at whose centre stood a deep attachment to continental liberalism in its intellectual and applied forms. Though such sentiments found a willing audience in turn of the century Ireland, they became anathema in the aftermath of the revolutionary events of 1916.

Kettle was far more complicated than this brief sketch can hope to convey, and his life does not fit neatly into a narrow revisionist rereading of modern Irish history. He presents a fascinating but highly frustrating subject for a biographer. It would be all too easy to write a biography of Kettle by Kettle, as his wit and astute characterisation make it almost impossible to resist quoting him at length. One is struck when reading the accounts of contemporaries how often he is remembered by a phrase, a joke or a one-liner. But, though his written work is lucid, it is by no means unambiguous. His views on a range of issues from constitutional politics to women's suffrage, from the tangled history of Anglo-Irish relations to Irish participation in the Great War, were both highly idiosyncratic and deeply theoretical. Like most politicians, he tailored his speeches to particular audiences, occasionally spoke on issues about which he had little more than cursory knowledge and sometimes disappointed his allies by changing his mind in the interests of political expediency. Unlike most politicians, however, he excelled at composition as well as oratory and his political writings were highly respected and widely read; his written legacy provides students of his political career with a wealth of information about his life and his times.

What is most striking, however, is the wall of secrecy that surrounds his personal life. Though this is by no means a psychological biography, it would be foolish to overlook the genesis and impact of his melancholic disposition, his frequent bouts of mysterious ill health and his alcoholism. Though it is abundantly clear that they played a major role in all aspects of his career, there is limited information about such matters in his private papers, just as there is very little extant information about his childhood or married life. Veiled references to his depression and alcoholism appear in memoirs and contemporary accounts, but his reputation was protected by powerful supporters and Victorian propriety; interestingly, even his political enemies – many of them highly skilled propagandists – tended to refer to his alcoholism in only the most oblique terms. His own frequent failure as a correspondent also contributed to the dearth of information about his private life. When a friend once threatened to write a 'Life and Times' of T. M. Kettle, Kettle retorted 'you will have no letters anyhow for I never write any'.[2] It is mainly through memoirs and remembrances, most of them written sometime after Kettle's death, that details of certain of his habits and idiosyncrasies emerge: his tardiness, his generosity, his love of practical jokes, his politeness to flower sellers, his obsession with Parnell and his love of good clothing are but a few.

This is not a full-scale 'life of' in the tradition of J. B. Lyons, from whose biography of Kettle I have learnt and borrowed much; there are necessarily a number of issues which are under-explored, the most obvious being Kettle's career as a poet and literary critic. I have also attempted to write a 'times of' as much as a 'life of', as the social and cultural environment of Kettle and his fellow middle-class Catholics at the *fin de siècle* is a lost world which historians have done little to recover. But most of all, this small book is intended to serve as an introduction to some of the lost ideas of Kettle's generation: to constitutional nationalism of course, but also to ideas about liberalism, cosmopolitanism, democracy and Europeanism. These are the ideas that shaped Kettle's life and death, ideas that continued to offer him consolation despite personal disappointments and the rising spectre of militarism that threatened to engulf his beloved Europe in the early years of the century. Kettle wrote and spoke on a wide variety of topics, but he was consistent in his conviction that Irish politics, history and culture belonged to and should be viewed within a European context. His translation of this from rhetoric into deed on the battlefields of France reminds one that the story of his life and his death reveals as much about the broader history of twentieth-century Europe as it does about the development of modern Ireland.

CHAPTER I

Family Life and Early Influences

Born on 9 February 1880 at Artane, County Dublin, Thomas Michael Kettle was the seventh of the twelve children of Andrew Kettle, a successful and respected farmer and a well-known political activist. Andrew Kettle owned holdings at Artane, St Margaret's and Malahide in County Dublin. He grew mostly barley, which he sold to distillers and brewers, but also kept some cattle and bred farm and road horses. He was a progressive and prosperous farmer who was hard working and intolerant of the laziness, sloppiness or feebleness occasionally displayed by his employees and children. He was also proud of his political and social origins, claiming in 1912 that 'I started in life as a ploughman on the family farm, and I have gloried in the dignity of labour ever since', and adding that he had resisted the temptation to emigrate during the Famine exodus of 1847 at the urging of his mother, 'the daughter of a '98 woman'.[1]

The Kettle family moved several times as it expanded, but most of the children were born at Millview in Malahide, and that 'long, rambling, two-storey house' was considered the family home.[2] Andrew Kettle's wife, Margaret McCourt of St Margaret's, County Dublin, was twenty years younger then her husband. A pious Catholic, she was also a 'self-effacing, colourless, kind' woman who sought 'refuge in the kitchen'.[3] Many of her household responsibilities seem to have been shared with her eldest daughter, Janie, who was something of a mother to her younger siblings.

Mrs Kettle appears to have been a harassed but much-loved mother whose children remained devoted to her.

According to Thomas, Andrew Kettle was known in every Irish home in the late nineteenth century. He had been active in the Tenant League in the 1850s and presided at the first meeting of the National Land League in 1879: he claimed in 1912 that 'few men have fought the Irish landlords like I have'.[4] A keen supporter and confidant of Charles Stewart Parnell, Kettle was instrumental in persuading him to become involved in the Land League. Parnell urged Kettle to stand for the Irish Parliamentary Party in 1880, but Kettle was defeated in the face of clerical opposition. A signatory to the radical 'No Rent Manifesto', Kettle's involvement in land agitation led to his imprisonment in 1881. He frequently published letters in the *Freeman's Journal*, and his loyalty to 'The Chief' ensured that he was respected until his death. It also provided Thomas Kettle with considerable political cachet when he embarked upon his own political career. Parnell and Napoleon were Andrew Kettle's heroes. He named one of his sons Charles Stewart and a daughter Josephine, and his children were brought up to revere Parnell in particular. Thomas Kettle's devotion to Parnell and the parliamentary cause has often been attributed to his father's influence, but his brother, Laurence, claimed that he and his siblings were less interested in politics than might have been expected.[5] They enjoyed the satirical verses Frank Hugh O'Donnell sent to their father and political visitors to their home made them aware of contemporary events though Andrew Kettle attempted to avoid exposing women and children to politics. He did, however, pass on to Thomas a love of literature, both modern and ancient; Kettle senior possessed a large library and was friendly with the writer Katharine Tynan. He was also a devout Catholic, who maintained that the Parnell incident was purely political. Thomas Kettle inherited his father's devotion and willingness to ignore clerical opinion when it contradicted his own.

Thomas Kettle rarely spoke of his childhood and family circumstances, but his brother and wife claimed that father and son enjoyed a close, although often tempestuous relationship.[6] After hearing of his son's death in 1916, Andrew Kettle was said to have exclaimed 'if Tom is dead I have no wish to live'. Though admired and largely obeyed, Andrew Kettle was also feared. A strict disciplinarian, he was described by one visitor to the Kettle home as 'autocratic' and a complete 'man's man'; 'he used to gather the men around him, and hoosh the women out of the room'. He presided over his family with an iron fist, even banishing his eldest son, Andy, from the family home after he jilted a local girl before marrying the daughter of a dentist. This broke Margaret Kettle's heart, and although Andy was her favourite, her husband refused to change his mind until just before he died. Tom Kettle found some solace in the homes of his friends, and particularly in the family home of his future wife, Mary Sheehy, which was warm and jolly and often full of visitors. Mary Sheehy noted that there were always 'wonderful meals' at the Kettle residence, with 'an enormous spread at high tea and dinner'.[7] Meals were much plainer at her own home, but though less prosperous than the Kettles, her family was much more sociable than her fiancé's, being known for its 'at homes' and frequent visitors. This was not lost on Tom Kettle, who declared in a letter to his sister: 'It seems to me that in our family more than any other I know there is an almost complete absence of that close and confidential intercourse which makes some homes so delightful. We are all too self-centred, and gloomy, and chill, and distrustful. It is a terrible fault.'

Kettle and his brothers were very well educated by the standards of the day. According to their fellow student and later Tom Kettle's close friend, Oliver St John Gogarty, they were sent daily in a 'governess trap' to the Christian Brothers' School in North Richmond Street.[8] The school had an excellent reputation and quite a mixed clientele, but the arrival of the Kettle brothers in the trap singled them out as 'the school taught the sons of working men for the most part'.[9] Although the Kettles performed well, their departure from the Brothers' school, which offered neither the academic nor social cachet required by a well-to-do family like their own, was almost inevitable. Tom and Laurence (Larry) Kettle were duly sent to Clongowes Wood College in County Kildare in 1894, Ireland's most prestigious Catholic school and Andrew Kettle's own *alma mater*. A boarding school, Clongowes provided the 14-year-old Kettle with his first sustained absence from his family and it was at Clongowes that his particular talents and interests became apparent. His friend, Arthur Clery, recalled that Kettle created a sensation at the school when he argued that the man who died on the battlefield died better than the man who died in his bed with the consolation of religion. This sentiment was seen to be risqué in the solidly Catholic environment of Clongowes, and Kettle was forced to recant.[10]

Sport played an important part in the life of Clongowes students and it is likely that the rural surroundings and excellent facilities for games pleased Kettle, an active and sporty child. He excelled as a cricketer, later claiming that the men who gave him business when he first went to the Bar were not his many political associates, but a few old cricketing friends.[11] He was also a keen cyclist, and with his brother founded a cycling club at the school. Gogarty claimed that Kettle's possession of a bicycle made him 'so envied' that tricks were played on him by schoolboy 'have nots'.[12] Kettle enjoyed wearing cycling shoes and knickerbockers and associating with like-minded sports enthusiasts at the college.[13] Sport was clearly important; such games as cricket and rugby signalled the social and economic standing of schools and their students, and a schoolboy's popularity and status often rested on his sporting prowess. Examination results, however, were still more important and came to dominate the lives of students. Clongowes students

contemporaries. He was also tall, handsome, urbane and well dressed; he was said to have asked a tailor to make him a 'new suit that would not look new and that, when old, would not look old'.[21] His leadership was widely acknowledged both then and later by his contemporaries such as William Fallon, who argued that Kettle was 'an idol, for he dominated the younger generation . . . as an essayist, poet, critic, nationalist and conversationalist and in addition he was a popular figure as an athlete, cyclist and footballer'.[22]

UCD provided Kettle with a platform and an ideal environment for the development of his political philosophy. The college stood at the heart of a prolonged debate about the establishment of a university which would be acceptable to the Catholic hierarchy and successive British governments. Many commentators argued that Catholic university students were poorly provided for, while their Protestant counterparts enjoyed the superior facilities offered by Trinity and the Queen's Colleges. Though Catholics were entitled to attend those institutions, most followed the clerical line and boycotted them. The alternative was the Royal University, an examining body which had the power to grant degrees to anybody who passed its examinations. A number of institutions served as *de facto* university colleges of the Royal, but UCD – the successor to Newman's old Catholic University – was considered to be the most prestigious. Like many of his fellow students, Kettle's relationship with the Royal University was an uneasy and highly political one. UCD students were aware that their very presence at the college constituted a political act, and the debate about university education helped the increasingly politicised UCD students to define their own role within the contemporary Irish social and political context. 'We knew', explained one student, 'that by coming to University College we were making a big sacrifice where Trinity had such prestige and the common life of a residential University. It intensified our national feelings.'[23] Unlike their Trinity counterparts, Kettle and his cohorts entered an institution which had been established barely a generation before, and which, owing to a lack of recognition and inadequate funding, had only just survived. Popularly known as the 'University Question', the issue provided an immediate and volatile opportunity for budding politicians like Kettle to transform rhetoric into political activism.

The University Question came to occupy much of Kettle's time at UCD, but his immediate concern was election to the college's Literary and Historical Society. The 'L&H', a debating society, had been revived by Francis Sheehy Skeffington during Kettle's first term at UCD and soon became a recognised training ground for a generation of would-be political leaders. In the organisation Kettle claimed to have found 'a home for my disaffection'.[24] He began to speak at L&H meetings almost immediately, and within a year of arriving at UCD he was elected president of the society. Kettle's controversial and flamboyant oratorical style was apparent from an early age, and the L&H gave him a chance to refine his skills. According to a fellow student, he was

> by no means an easy or pleasant speaker. The intonation with which the public were later to become familiar, sounded affected in a boy of eighteen, while the sarcasm and irony which were to delight and hurt legislative assemblies and listening multitudes in days to come, grated rather in those early days.[25]

Delivered in November 1898, Kettle's inaugural address, 'The Celtic Revival', presented a summary of his developing political beliefs. At first glance the title appears to be little more than topical; the cultural revival was, after all, gaining supporters among young middle-class Catholics, the very constituency Kettle's address was delivered to. His speech was, however, rather unfashionable in the context of the devastation which had befallen the Irish Parliamentary Party and the seemingly endless years of

Conservative rule. Encouraged by the growth of the United Irish League (UIL) and changes in local government, Kettle emphasised the primacy of constitutional political activity to the regeneration of the nation; as his close friend, Constantine Curran, explained, for Kettle the Celtic Revival 'meant the revival of Celtic literature, but much more the revival of the Celt'.[26] His assertion that art would always play an important but supporting role in the process of the rejuvenation of the nation was one which he would return to often during his political career; his inaugural address provided a taste of his increasingly uneasy relationship with the Gaelic League and Irish cultural revivalism in general.

Kettle was known as an 'O'Growneyite', a member of the UCD set who walked about with copies of Fr O'Growney's *Simple Lessons in Irish* protruding from their pockets. But as Fallon later claimed, Kettle had misgivings, arguing 'here we are learning Irish on the threshold of becoming accomplished speakers of English'.[27] His wife maintained that 'as a good linguist' Kettle had mastered Irish 'to a very high degree' by 1916 and that he planned, upon his return from the front, to translate two poems into Irish. If Kettle did master the Irish language, he kept this particular skill largely to himself. He never condemned the language movement *per se* and even claimed that most of the younger members of the Irish Parliamentary Party had joined the Gaelic League, but he consistently denied the notion that language was a requisite for nationality and decried the tendency of language enthusiasts to aggrandise their cause at the expense of practical politics.

His view of Gaelicism became more dogged in later years, unsurprising for a profoundly liberal man who eschewed both compulsion and anti-modernity. This placed him in an exclusive clique of UCD students who became critics of the Gaelic League for a variety of reasons. Fellow devotees of the Irish Party like J. J. Horgan – an active member of the Gaelic League – shared his belief in the primacy of constitutional politics, while James Joyce similarly condemned the movement's provincialism and prescriptive tendencies. But it was Francis Sheehy Skeffington, close friend, fellow maverick and subsequently his brother-in-law when he married Hanna Sheehy, in whom he found a soulmate and a political ally. A fellow patron of the L&H, Sheehy Skeffington was not yet as committed to socialism as he would later become and, during his student days, was an ardent supporter of the IPP. When Kettle and Sheehy Skeffington collaborated on the editorship of the political journal, the *Nationist*, in 1905, authoritarian Gaelicism became one of their primary targets, though they did publish poems in Irish and supported Irish manufacture and cultural pursuits. In private life the activities of enthusiastic Irish-Ireland movement proved to be the basis of a shared cynicism and source of amusement.

Kettle's university career was interrupted by ill health, which forced him to resign from the L&H and fail to sit the Bachelor of Arts examination in 1900. The precise nature of his illness remains a mystery, though it is likely that he suffered a nervous breakdown. His wife later claimed that 'over-study had strained his nervous system, and he never quite regained normal health';[28] passages in his diaries and notebooks reveal a melancholy streak and a deep pessimism. Robert Lynd wrote that Kettle seemed to 'go about visibly accompanied by doom. His conversation at times was like a comment on doom, scornful, cheerful, challenging, paradoxical – emotion turned back from the abyss with an epigram.'[29] Kettle himself described life rather morosely as 'a cheap table d'hôte in a rather dirty restaurant, with Time changing the plates before you have had enough of everything'.[30] He spent some of this year in Europe, visiting France, Germany and Belgium and improving his German and French. But his gloomy disposition continued to worry his friends and family. In 1901, his exasperated and concerned brother asked him 'Why, oh why will you ever assume such a pessimistic attitude in your letters? It makes me feel uncomfortable for a week after.'[31]

His delicate health was compromised again in 1904 by the death of his beloved brother, William, 'a veritable twin soul'. His wife claimed that this 'sorrow, together with his shattered nerves was responsible for his somewhat tragic and melancholy temperament'.[32] He travelled once more to the continent, this time spending a year reading philosophy and history at Innsbruck University. His time away improved both his German and his health. Notwithstanding the 'new and trying diet', his body was stretched by physical exercise. He told his sister Janie that 'three weeks ago in Dublin I was in a state of the most frightful collapse, two days ago in Innsbruck I was hardly better, but yesterday in the mountains I felt like a new man'. He concluded his letter, however, with a request for her prayers, admitting that while he was in 'splendid condition' that day, he suffered 'much longer spells of blacked depression'.[33]

A dedicated cosmopolitan and talented linguist, Kettle continued, while abroad, to read widely in modern European literature and philosophy and was later to translate L. F. A. Paul-Dubois's *Contemporary Ireland* and contribute an introduction to the translation from French of Daniel Halévy's *Life of Frederick Nietzsche*. His time abroad had a profound effect both on his general political views and particularly his views about Ireland. His insistence that internationalism complemented and reinforced nationalism was to earn him the enmity of some Irish-Irelanders and advanced nationalists, as was his refusal to engage in a narrow form of nationalism which held that 'because a thing is English it is necessarily vile'. Neither did he maintain that all things Irish were necessarily worthy. 'He was', according to Dawson, 'national in his soul and cosmopolitan in his outlook. Insularity and provincialism had no part in his composition.'[34]

But Kettle's life consisted of more than politics and youthful angst. Contemporary accounts of life at UCD suggest a vibrant student culture and plenty of distractions from academic life. Recitals and poetry readings were popular forms of entertainment, and many of Kettle's contemporaries were avid theatregoers as well. Cycling, football and tennis were widely enjoyed, and walking parties were especially favoured by health-conscious students such as Sheehy Skeffington, who was said to have walked from Dublin to Glendalough in one day – a distance of sixty miles.[35] Less puritanical scholars were also known to frequent brothels in Tyrone Street. The difficulties involved in attending a poor university with little collegiate life also facilitated a student culture fostered by a lively social life. Though some students could live at home while they studied, many lived in lodgings rather than halls of residence. Walks between the college and various digs supplied numerous opportunities for informal discussions and debates, especially after Saturday evening meetings of the L&H. Moreover, the college's lack of an adequate library led to the National Library of Ireland becoming an informal student centre and meeting place for the many students scattered throughout the various colleges affiliated to the Royal University. Students who engaged in lively debates in the main reading room were likely to be asked to leave by the librarian, Mr Lyster, but they were often resumed on the library's front steps, a particularly popular forum for discussion. Most of the readers were young men from University College and the Cecelia St Medical School, but frequent and welcome readers also included the female students from Alexandra College, St Mary's University College and the Dominican Convent in Eccles Street. Despite some clerical opposition, female students had become involved in some aspects of UCD life, including compiling a 'girl graduates' chat' column in the college journal and hard-won membership of the L&H. It is hardly surprising that a number of young UCD men – including Kettle and Sheehy Skeffington – married women they met through college friends and societies.

The fierce debates which accompanied the attempts of women to gain admission to the L&H mirrored many of the controversies launched and no doubt enjoyed by UCD students. Another source of almost constant debate and amusement was the place in the college of the Irish language. George Clancy, a friend of Kettle's and later mayor of Limerick (who was to be shot dead by Black and Tans in 1921), introduced a branch of the Gaelic League to the college in 1898. Though Clancy was himself a dedicated Irish-Irelander, many of the people he persuaded to take Irish lessons – including Kettle and Joyce – did so out of curiosity or academic interest rather than political conviction. Neither Joyce nor Kettle persevered with Irish for very long. Joyce, who was taught by Patrick Pearse, became tired of his teacher's denigration of the English language, and particularly his denouncement of the word 'thunder' as an 'example of verbal inadequacy'; this was, it seems, one of Joyce's favourite words.[36]

Joyce's own contribution to university debates, most famously his defence of Ibsen and attempts to deliver a paper entitled 'Drama and Life' at a meeting of the L&H, also added spice to the college environment. The college rector, William Delany, blocked his first attempt, and when permission was finally granted he found himself attacked by Arthur Clery, Hugh Kennedy and others for his alleged hostility towards religion and nationalism. Kettle was one of the few who defended Joyce and subsequently wrote a favourable (though not uncritical) review of *Chamber Music*; however, he later refused to support the publication of *Dubliners*, which he deemed far too outspoken and quite possibly libellous.

Joyce himself was known at UCD as 'dreaming Jimmy' or 'the Hatter', but he could give as good as he got. For example, he described Sheehy Skeffington as 'Knickerbockers' because he wore plus fours, and 'Hairy Jaysus' after he grew a beard in protest against shaving. A number of the turn-of-the-century UCD set eventually appeared in Joyce's novels: George Clancy as Davin and Madden; John Francis Byrne as Cranly; Sheehy Skeffington as McCann and Fr Delany as the Rev. Dr Dillon. Joyce also immortalised Mary Sheehy, basing his Emma Clery in *Stephen Hero* on this young woman who captured his attention before she married Kettle. Mary Sheehy's family home at Belvedere Place became central to the social life of a number of UCD students, including Kettle, Joyce and Sheehy Skeffington. The family hosted an 'at home' on the second Saturday of each month with popular amusements such as dancing, singing and charades. Mary Sheehy's father, David, was a former nationalist MP, Fenian sympathiser and Land League advocate; her Uncle Eugene had been imprisoned in 1881 and was commonly known as the 'Land League Priest'; her sister, Hanna, was a prominent feminist and nationalist in her own right. The mixture of joviality and seriousness found in the Sheehy home reflected wider student culture: almost every form of amusement was in some way touched by politics, be it language classes, theatre-going, singing or even sport. This was precisely the kind of environment in which Kettle could flourish.

Meanwhile, Kettle was also learning to flourish in other environments, most notoriously in bars and hotels. A favourite meeting place was the Bailey, a haunt of Dublin intellectuals including Gogarty and James Stephens, and politicians such as Arthur Griffith. He subsequently became a frequent visitor to the United Arts Club, where his charm ensured that 'the male members could not leave his company'.[37] Though Kettle's serious drinking did not begin while he was at university, he was no doubt influenced by the excesses of fellow students including Joyce and Gogarty, and drawn to the conviviality found among fellow wits whose tongues had been loosened by alcohol. But his behaviour evidently remained more respectable – or his excesses better hidden – than his peers' for some time: Gogarty's own mother begged Kettle to help her 'counteract the bad effects' of her son's allegedly agnostic artistic and literary friends,[38] believing that the 'great respect' in which Oliver Gogarty held Kettle would enable him to steer her son down a purer path.[39]

As much as he enjoyed student debates and entertainments, Ketle had a living to make and the obvious choice was the law. After returning to Ireland and taking his Bachelor of Arts in mental and moral science in 1902, Kettle entered the King's Inns as a law student. This did not, however, lead to a break with UCD. He co-founded the Cui Bono Club, an exclusive college dining society composed mainly of lawyers and law students, which debated topical and often controversial issues. Distinguished fellow members included Hugh Kennedy (later Chief Justice of the Irish Free State), Marcus O'Sullivan (future Free State Minister of Education), and Arthur Clery (future Professor of Law at UCD). Kettle presided over the club, managing to bring together people of varying political and religious backgrounds while keeping the atmosphere at meetings friendly. He was, in the opinion of Clery,

> the Johnson of the Club, its acknowledged dictator and wit. In such circumstances his brilliant parts showed at their best – his lambent humour, his clever dialectic, his extraordinary personal charm, his marvellous skill in telling a story. Most of its members were clever men with distinguished careers, but Kettle was the sun of the firmament.[40]

Kettle's appealing personal style won many friends and admirers, but it also likely helped to mask his frequent bouts of melancholy self-doubt. When assessing the success of the Cui Bono, he confessed to Curran that

The great danger was that knowing each other so well we should lapse a little too much into chaff and gossip. I fear we have done so. On looking back on our meetings I find that I personally have as a rule brought my own thoughts to meetings and brought them back very little changed. Clery tells me that it is mainly my own fault and that my dictatorial and overriding manner prevents people from communicating to me what they know and I do not know. Heaven only knows how far the said manner is from conveying the real state of my mind which is full of nothing save bewilderment and ignorance and inaccurate glimpses and vain velleities and half-grasped conceptions which I lack energy either of mind or body to carry out . . . For myself wondering here alone, turning over the ashes of my life in which I seek fruitlessly for any ideal thread, tossed between vain ambition and this gnawing distress of brain and nerve which cancels everything, I feel coming home to me for the first time in all its urgency 'the grimness of the general human situation'. I feel the need of discipline, of desperate sincerity; I feel life overcoming me, and cannot solve the problem of earning my daily bread.[41]

Kettle nonetheless joined a great many clubs and societies including the Academy of Thomas Aquinas, an association devoted to the discussion of philosophical questions. Like so many of the organisations with which he was associated during his time at UCD, the Academy boasted an impressive list of members including Michael Gill, Felix Hackett and Thomas Bodkin. Whether or not James Joyce joined the society remains questionable, but it seems that Kettle was the only student with whom Joyce would discuss Aquinas. In common with many of his cohorts, Kettle remained true to his Catholic upbringing, continuing to attend mass and enjoying cordial relations with a number of priests including the Archbishop of Dublin, William Walsh, who had 'taken a great fancy to him'.[42]

Kettle remained involved with the L&H and in 1903 became editor of *St Stephen's*, a UCD student newspaper established in 1901. *St Stephen's* had forged a reputation for wit, humour and political commentary. Clery, a regular contributor to the paper, claimed that three schools of thought flourished in Ireland between the fall of Parnell and the rise of Sir Edward Carson: constitutional nationalism, the Irish-Ireland movement and an 'aspiration towards modern progress of the less brutal kind'.[43] *St Stephen's* published articles that espoused all three creeds, but a combination of the first and last predominated under Kettle's editorship. Of primary importance was the University Question, an issue which assumed greater importance in the college after the publication of the Final Report of the Commissioners on University Education in 1903. Along with a number of fellow students including Patrick Pearse, Arthur Clery and Con Curran, Kettle had joined the Catholic Graduates' and Undergraduates' Association which was dedicated to securing improved facilities for Catholic university students. Through *St Stephen's* he pursued this theme, arguing that 'Orange opposition to Catholic wants' should not stand in the way of a favourable settlement.[44] The Commission failed to establish the endowed Catholic University or University College that the Catholic hierarchy and its supporters had hoped for, and by 1905 Kettle and other student activists took a more vigorous approach to the University Question. No longer content with merely issuing statements, the students began to display their dissatisfaction with the prevailing system, sometimes in an unorthodox fashion.

Student dissidents had disturbed degree-giving ceremonies of the Royal University in the 1880s and 1890s, but never so spectacularly as in 1905 when Kettle was named by the University Senate as one of the ringleaders of a circle of students who occupied the organ gallery during a conferring ceremony at Earlsfort Terrace. Students disrupted the ceremony with renditions of 'God Save

Ireland', and serenaded the university senators as they left the building. Kettle was summoned to a meeting of the Standing Committee, but denied involvement in the incident and threatened both legal action and to burn his Royal University degree. Kettle in fact took no part in the event at the Royal University, but earned considerable publicity from the episode. The incident allowed him another opportunity to expand his views on the University Question and on the anomalous position of the Royal University. 'Your university', read his letter to the university Senate, 'is not a university in the true sense of the word.' This was a theme he was to pursue during his political career, losing no opportunity to extol the virtues of UCD while making clear his opposition to the Royal University. In 1907, for example, he explained to the House of Commons that the Royal University buildings were used for numerous purposes when not required for university business and amused his audience with the following story to illustrate his objection:

A couple of years ago a friend of mine who was awarded a medal for English verse went there for an examination. He said to the hall porter, 'What institution is this?' The porter replied, 'You know very well it is the Royal University of Ireland.' 'Well', said his friend, 'the last time I was round here it was a flower show.'[45]

At a rally held by UCD students at Stephen's Green, Kettle defended the students' right to protest, as the Royal University 'was simply a paper corporation with an occasional existence from examination to examination'. He denied that the demonstration had offered a personal insult to the king, emphasising instead the political motive behind the disturbance.[46] The incident was reported widely in the Irish and British press, enhancing his standing within nationalist circles and generally augmenting his reputation among the reading public. His talent for publicity and public speaking had become especially apparent during the short-lived controversy, valuable assets for a man who appeared increasingly bent on a political career. His earlier awkwardness had been replaced by a confidence and flair that earned him a reputation as a formidable and impressive orator. Fellow students remembered his imposing presence and wit as a speaker, describing him as 'a born orator', who later 'took his natural place as a debater with giants like Balfour, Asquith and John Redmond'.[47]

Privately, he characteristically made light of the 'organ affair', asking Curran, the following year: 'Have arrangements been made to blow up the organ at Earlsfort Terrace? Please send me a fragment.'[48] This kind of quip was typical of Kettle, who was known for his quick wit and love of practical jokes. He indulged in the latter while a law student at the King's Inns and even after he was called to the bar. On one memorable occasion, having been required to drink a toast to the health of the king at a formal event at the Inns, a disgruntled and indignant Kettle and his fellow nationalists entered the following limerick into the Attendance Book:

> We six of us dined at the Inns
> Of liquors we sampled the bins
> They proposed the King's health
> And we drank it – by stealth
> May Ireland forgive us our sins[49]

The majority of Kettle's early twentieth-century contemporaries supported the Irish Parliamentary Party and its aim to win Home Rule by constitutional means. But they were no more immune from the impact of the 'new nationalism' than other young, middle-class Irish men and women. Kettle was no exception. He, like many of his university friends, read a number of the small periodicals such as D. P. Moran's *Leader* and Arthur Griffith's

United Irishman which were at that time causing a small stir in nationalist circles. In common with a number of prominent Irish-Irelanders, Kettle was appalled by Yeats's *Countess Cathleen* when it was performed in 1899, and was one of the 30 UCD students who signed a letter of protest against the play's depiction of Irish life and Irish peasants, objecting to the representation of 'the Irish peasant as a crooning barbarian, crazed with morbid superstition who having added the Catholic faith to his store of superstition sells that faith for gold or bread in the proving of famine'.[50] Constantine Curran believed that Kettle was the likely author of the letter, and certainly much of its phrasing and imagery bears his stamp.[51] Like a number of other critics, Kettle remained suspicious of Yeats's depiction of the 'real Ireland', and deplored his characterisation of Catholic Irish peasants.[52] A budding poet himself, Kettle later published some of his own poetry in the *United Irishman*; he also produced 'Mr Yeats and the Freedom of the Theatre', a reflective review of W. B. Yeats's works for the Griffithite newspaper in 1902 in which he once again challenged the poet's characterisation of Irish Catholics.[53] He did not contest Yeats's right to write about Catholicism, but insisted that he had misrepresented it. He later admitted that Yeats had done 'some good' in his attempt to create a national literature.[54]

His fascination with new political ideas and movements was not narrowly restricted to Irish concerns. He read continental philosophy and was, for a short time, dedicated to Nietzsche who, he claimed, 'made German dance before him as only Heine had done'. Given his interest in new political ideas and Continental movements, it is hardly surprising that he enjoyed a mild flirtation with socialism at this time. With Francis Sheehy Skeffington, Maurice Joy and Frederick Ryan he planned the establishment of a 'National Democratic Committee' which would link the aims of the British Labour Party and the anticlericalism of Michael Davitt.[55]

By 1912, however, he had abandoned any such support, declaring that 'the whole tradition of Europe' was 'against Socialism'.[56]

Kettle continued to write and contemplate alternative political ideas, but he remained first and foremost a devotee of constitutional politics and what he believed to be the associated notions of progress and pragmatism. His early pronouncements on the University Question had hinted at both his ambition to become involved at a high level with policy formation and his determination to apply modern and imaginative approaches to Irish concerns. From 1904–5, however, not only did he dedicate himself with increasing zeal to the Irish Party, but applied himself, his biting wit and caustic humour to denouncing its challengers on what he described as the 'Extreme Right of Nationalism, the Separatists'.

His primary target became the kind of separatism typified by Sinn Féin, but his denunciation of this organisation was more complex and gradual than has sometimes been allowed. Kettle's friends testified that he flirted in his youth with Griffith's ideas and the loose conglomeration of advanced nationalist organisations which formed the nucleus of the emerging Sinn Féin. It fact, Kettle greeted the publication of Griffith's *Resurrection of Hungary* with great enthusiasm, claiming that it supplied the separatist wing with a much-needed 'political policy'.[57] The treatise was read and analysed by Kettle at the Cui Bono; Griffith himself was in the audience at Kettle's invitation and was treated to his 'acute but not unfriendly analysis' of his treatise.[58] His first major piece on Griffith's Hungarian policy was published in 1905 and its title, 'Would the Hungarian Policy Work?', is a good indication of Kettle's early reservations about Griffith's project. He acknowledged that the Irish Parliamentary Party had waned since the 'debacle of '93', and he praised the *United Irishman* for its good work in promoting the Irish language, literature and industry. More importantly, however, it was in his analysis of the pamphlet and in the questions he raised about it that we can see the exposition of what was to be his single most constant political appeal: the necessity for all shades of Irish nationalism to present a united front and pursue a common goal. In common with so many activists of his generation, the earlier fragmentation of the Irish Party, for him, represented the nadir of nationalist politics. A return to the dismal 1890s was unthinkable; twentieth-century nationalism had to be both revitalised and fortified if it was to avoid the same ignoble fate. The publication of *The Resurrection of Hungary* was to be welcomed because it suggested that nationalism itself was being nourished by new ideas, a new commitment and a new vigour.

Kettle's approval of the pamphlet indicated his general attraction to new ideas and programmes; this in turn reflected both his openness to modern thought and, perhaps more importantly, his genuine search at this time for a new political orthodoxy which could be applied in a constructive and methodical way to the Irish situation. For Kettle, the early years of the twentieth century were a time of contemplation and preparation for the political life for which he seemed destined. While it was clear to him that the old party orthodoxy was no longer sufficient, he maintained that crucial aspects of the old party machinery and ideology should not be ditched, for they represented what Kettle came to describe as 'realism in politics'. Some, though by no means all, of his youthful idealism began to dissolve as he increasingly embraced the party which, he argued, possessed the experience, machinery and results necessary to secure Home Rule for Ireland.[59]

Central to Kettle's vision of Ireland under Home Rule was a fully functioning democracy whose institutions were based on British models. Like Westminster, College Green was to house governments and oppositions whose political outlooks were to be based on a wide set of issues rather than on Home Rule alone. With its disciplined structure, its constituency organisations and its commitment to constitutional politics, the party represented for him a blueprint of the kind of institutions which would flourish in a modern and democratic Ireland. He argued that while there would be no need for a Home Rule party in College Green, there would be room for new political parties that would similarly engage with electors and the Irish legislature. In other words, Ireland would face the same kinds of issues and debates as other modern nations whose political destinies were decided by democratically elected governments. He claimed on many occasions that such issues were likely to be complex and controversial and that Home Rule should not be viewed as a panacea or as an excuse to avoid discussion of questions other than Ireland's constitutional position: 'Assuredly, we must not seem to suggest that in an autonomous Ireland public life will be all nougat, velvet, and soft music. There will be conflicts, and vehement conflicts, for that is the way of the twentieth century.'[60]

Thus, though Kettle could describe Griffith's *Resurrection of Hungary* as a 'brilliant pamphlet', he denied that it offered an achievable political strategy or a realistic political model. He outlined two main objections: the fact that the pamphlet read 'like a fairy tale', and that 'the writer hardly realised the magnitude of his suggestion, and does not develop it in sufficient detail to justify a prudent man either in accepting or in rejecting it'. He noted that Griffith showed 'extreme impatience with those who are unwilling forthwith to abandon the traditions of a century in favour of a new adventure' and urged the policy's exponents to 'realise the vastness of their project' and 'the need for exact designs'.[61] When Gogarty, a friend and supporter of Griffith, approached Kettle in the hope of convincing him to 'join Griffith and help him to found a party that would withdraw from Westminster', Kettle listened 'with patience and politeness' before proceeding to 'expose at once the weakness and danger of Griffith's policy'.[62]

Given his own fascination with European history and intellectual currents, Kettle cannot have failed to be enthused by Griffith's use of a continental model. On the other hand, his careful mind became increasingly offended by Griffith's imprecision and opportunistic borrowings from cultures and situations he did not take the trouble to understand in any great depth. As Bulmer Hobson pointed out, there were many violent attacks made on the Hungarian parallel, and Kettle's concerns about Hungarian history and Griffith's technical points were shared by other critics as well.[63] But Kettle's main aim at this time was not to denounce Griffith's movement; rather, he urged co-operation with the constitutionalists. 'There is nothing', he argued, 'in the nature of things to prevent our Separatists and "Constitututionalists", our *Nationalists* and *Nationists* – if I may invent a word – from co-operating as Kossuth co-operated with Szechenyi and Deák, as Davis with O'Connell.'[64]

But co-operation was one thing and capitulation was another. Kettle was not to pursue this accommodating approach for much longer. Sinn Féin had not yet evolved into the identifiable political grouping with a pronounced policy of anti-constitutionalism which it would become; many considered it in 1905 to be merely one of a growing number of small and interesting new nationalist organisations. If Griffith and his supporters intensified their hostility towards the Irish Party, Kettle would be among the first to denounce them. Consequently, his article sounded a few warning notes, particularly in relation to the South Mayo by-election of 1900. This election was the scene of an unpleasant struggle between members of Griffith's circle and the United Irish League. John MacBride – hero of the Irish pro-Boers – was nominated by Griffith, Maud Gonne and other members of the Irish Transvaal Committee to stand as a candidate in the by-election. The party and the United Irish League had opposed MacBride, and this served to sour further relations between the organisations. Kettle had himself opposed the Boer War and had distributed anti-recruitment leaflets, but he maintained his conviction that elections should be fought by the experienced Irish Party and not by well-meaning but unskilled amateurs who could do nothing but split the nationalist vote.

In an article published in 1908, he pursued his argument that the Irish Party was the most likely of all nationalist groups to deliver Irish autonomy, not surprisingly since he was a nationalist MP at the time. At his polemical and political best, he made reference to authorities as diverse as Spinoza, Herbert Spencer, John Redmond and the 'Dublin lady who, mistaking the Irish for French, called it the "Sans Fin" policy, the policy without end'; 'she spoke', he claimed, 'with a wisdom deeper than her own'. He warned Sinn Féin supporters to remember that politics was 'not a matter of abstract ideas but of concrete proposals' and argued that 'you push the policy of withdrawal too far when you withdraw not merely from Westminster but also from the ballot boxes of Ireland'. He denied claims that Irish parliamentarians grew fat on the salaries paid by gullible Irish supporters – a common accusation repeatedly levelled by Griffith. And, no doubt knowing that Griffith himself attached a deep significance to Parnell, he argued that 'Parnell went to Westminster, and what was good enough for Parnell is good enough for us'. Unsurprisingly, Griffith and Kettle would later wrangle over the legacy of the Chief.

Perhaps the most interesting part of his 1908 essay is the section where he addressed the larger question of separatism – attaching to it an almost mystical quality, but refusing to state precisely where he stood on the issue – and in the process revealing the basis of his own developing animosity towards Sinn Féin:

Sinn Féin . . . has been created out of the will and mind of one man, Mr Arthur Griffith, whose strength is only less conspicuous than his narrowness. Mr Griffith began some ten years ago as the leader of the 'physical force' remnant. Whether that word 'remnant' has anything of an Arnoldian sense I do not care to say: but Parliamentary Nationalists have always regarded them as the keepers of an ideal, the priests of a mystery, the guardians of a temple that must be conserved. Sovereign independence for Ireland, undoubtedly, makes an appeal to the imagination which is not made by Home Rule. The right of a nation to seek freedom by force of arms must be asserted, though there be no opportunity of putting it into action. Such is the inspiration behind the extremist ideal; no Irishman has ever refused his respect to it; and for that and other reasons there existed a relation of friendship and tolerance between Mr Griffith's group and us until the General Election of 1900. Then there was a misunderstanding. It grew less and less bridgeable; and in a little while Mr Griffith found himself committed to bitter hostility to the Parliamentary party. He groped about for three or four years in a purely negative fashion.[65]

The IPP had long included a range of opinions, which stretched from republicanism to a variety of nationalism that demanded merely the mildest form of political separation from the United Kingdom. Kettle believed that part of Parnell's genius had been to allow such a diversity of outlooks to coexist within a disciplined political party which made a real impact on ballot boxes while continuing to extol the virtues of – and lay claim to the legacy of – separatists like Wolfe Tone. This was hardly a new sentiment; occasions such as the centenary celebrations of the 1798 Rebellion had seen Redmond and Dillon eulogising Tone while urging crowds to support constitutional politics. Kettle was as aware as his senior colleagues that, while the political aspirations of nineteenth-century Irish radicals had not won mass support, funerals, oratory and pageantry had caught the attention of nationalist Ireland. In a culture where political martyrdom continued to impress and inspire, wholesale condemnation of the 'separatist spirit' would win him few friends. A careful cultivation of the vitality of Fenianism with the realities of practical politics became one of his trademarks. As he told a largely English audience:

> I wish to say frankly that although I have had Fenian forerunners, although I have refused to dismiss from my regard the names of men who in the old days fought to tear down your flag, I have no desire to separate from Great Britain. I consider that Home Rule for the first time will be a union between the two countries.[66]

His admiration for elements of various strands of Irish nationalism was reflected in his selection in 1915 of a number of speeches that were published as *Irish Orators and Oratory*. Tone, Emmet and the Manchester Martyrs featured, but so too did A. M. Sullivan, Isaac Butt and John Redmond. Predictably, his hero, Charles Stewart Parnell, was awarded the most pages, and the chosen addresses were among Parnell's more moderate utterances. They featured denials of the existence of formal links between the Irish Party and the Irish Republican Brotherhood, a defence of constitutional Home Rule and, more topically, acclaim for the fighting skills of Irish soldiers.[67]

By the time of the publication of his Sinn Féin article in 1908, Kettle had entered parliament and clashed with Sinn Féiners on a number of occasions. It would be wrong to try to pinpoint the exact moment when Kettle's political opinion turned so decisively in the direction of constitutional politics, for the shift was neither sudden nor uncomplicated. It is clear that he had been an ardent supporter of the Irish Parliamentary Party from an early age and it is equally plain that most of his flirtation with advanced nationalism was both highly qualified and ephemeral. As Arthur Clery noted, 'Kettle was at all relevant times a constitutionalist'.[68] The party had been an important part of his life since boyhood, not least because of his father's deep and continuing involvement in constitutional politics. Father and son together helped to inaugurate the North Dublin Executive of the UIL in 1902, Kettle Junior serving as its secretary.[69] As a member of the UIL Directory, Kettle attended most of its important meetings and functions, and a place at the centre of party politics appeared increasingly likely. From late 1904 he began to lay the path that would subsequently lead to a political career and attendant ideology on the one hand more established, and on the other always unpredictable. He had published a number of literary reviews and short pieces, but after his return from Europe in 1904 his written output became steadier and more concerned with Irish questions. Freed from the pressure of studying, he began to contribute articles and reviews to a number of journals and newspapers. As Kettle became better known within nationalist and artistic circles, the political career for which he seemed destined looked to be increasingly within his reach.

CHAPTER 2

Political Apprenticeship

In 1906 Kettle was called to the Bar, having served as auditor of the Literary and Historical Society and having won both the L&H Gold Medal for Oratory and the Victoria Prize at King's Inn. His legal career was not, however, destined to flourish. He rarely accepted cases and, on the rare occasions when he could be persuaded to don his robes, they were inevitably political, most famously when he defended several cattle drivers in 1907.[1] His wife claimed that he would have been an unhappy lawyer because he was 'too sensitive', and it appears that he disliked practising law and found the judicial system intellectually and morally dubious.[2] Despite his cynicism, to many of his friends at least he had the stature and the intellectual and oratorical flair which separated merely capable barristers from the brilliant practitioners of their profession. And though he hardly practised, Kettle used his professional status as a dialectic prop on a number of occasions, including in 1916 when he considered the problem of partition from a lawyer's perspective:

> If a very needy and somewhat dishonest individual owed you £32, and when you proceeded to sue him you found that he had squared the judge and packed the jury, but at the last moment he offered you £26 on account, what ought you to do? I am but a poor lawyer, but I should strongly advise you to accept the money without prejudice.[3]

If Kettle was not to make his living practising law, what career paths were open to him? A seemingly never-ending stream of bright young men armed with BAs and ambition but without a clear professional path was an all too common sight in turn-of-the-century Ireland. Like a number of his UCD contemporaries, Kettle managed to combine professional life with political activism and occasional journalism; he wrote for the *New Ireland Review*, which was edited by his friend and former UCD tutor, Fr Tom Finlay, and starting in 1904 he began to contribute more or less regularly to the *Freeman's Journal*. He was no doubt aided by the unofficial patronage network, which helped to lubricate the transition from the university to professional life, and political allegiances often played a part in informal canvassing for professional support. But, as Kettle and his friends were to find, this strategy left them open to accusation of jobbery and place-hunting; this became particularly savage when Kettle subsequently sought support for his candidature for the professorship of National Economics at UCD.

In the early years of the century Kettle moved towards a more settled political career. He was acutely aware of the impatience with which the younger generation viewed the Irish Party and, more importantly, of the untapped talent which the organisation continued to ignore. Surrounded as he was by a number of able and politically active young men and women who were increasingly turning to organisations like Sinn Féin and the Gaelic League, he became determined to reinvigorate the party and to establish its relevance in twentieth-century Ireland by harnessing some of their new found enthusiasm. 'He was', as one commentator noted, 'early aware of the restiveness of the young men and of the necessity of supplying them with a place in the National movement before they chose one for themselves.'[4] At a public meeting presided over by Joseph Devlin in November 1904, the Young Ireland Branch of the United Irish League was formed, Kettle playing the leading

role in its establishment. Kettle spoke at this first meeting, emphasising the devastating impact on the constitutional movement of
the Parnell split, and pledging to breathe new life into the party.
When the Young Ireland Branch – usually known as the YIB –
reconvened in December, Kettle was elected president and he
immediately attracted a formidable group of like-minded young
men and women to the fledgling organisation.

The YIB has often been described as a ginger group, a youthful
version of the more staid UIL branches. Such an assessment is
accurate up to a point, but fails to capture the unconventionality of
the YIB membership. The organisation was undoubtedly allied to
the UIL and the Irish Parliamentary Party, but it remained a distinct
identity, and was unallied to any ward or parish as UIL branches
usually were.[5] Had members like Kettle and Sheehy Skeffington
been satisfied with a mere supporting role, they would surely have
been content with their local UIL groups, but both men found a
natural home in the company of their progressive contemporaries.
The YIB stated that no distinction of 'sex, class or creed' would be
placed on membership, and its early adherents included men and
women who had already been engaged with nonconformist politics:
Hanna and Francis Sheehy Skeffington were known for their
espousal of various causes including feminism and anti-vivisec-
tion; a number, including Kettle, had opposed the Boer War; a
growing number embraced cultural nationalism, while most had
been involved in university politics. Of the latter group, Cruise
O'Brien – later Kettle's brother-in-law when he married Kathleen
Sheehy – was especially well known, no doubt in part because he
was often referred to as 'The Pocket Yeats' due to his alleged
resemblance to the poet, but also because he was so heavily and
seriously implicated in student protests at the Royal University
conferring ceremonies. YIBs self-consciously presented themselves
as unorthodox, modern, and as no mere slavish followers of the

Irish Party; in the words of one member, the YIB revolted 'against the party machine'.[6] In the words of another, 'youth was more conspicuous than unity' in the YIB whose membership included constitutionalists, Gaelicists and near separatists.[7] What bound them was a fierce commitment to Home Rule which owed more to the memory of the radical Parnellite years than it did to the policy of Redmond, and a strong belief that while the party was salvageable, the old political order was simply that – old. Kettle seemed to many to be the only man who could reconcile the aspirations of the young nationalists with a party which seemed not only to be losing touch with the younger generation, but to be deliberately turning its back on the new ideas which enthused them. As Shane Leslie argued:

> He seemed destined to fulfil a vital but never quite attainable part in Irish life, to reconcile the old generation of Parliamentarians with the new Ireland which had arisen to demand better things . . . his friends were the young Irelanders who were already breaking in sympathy with the Irish party. He alone could have wrought a reconciliation and possibly averted the terrible revolt which buried so much promise in the ruins of Dublin.[8]

A combination of a sentimental yearning for the good old days when the Irish Party had seemed to wield real political power at Westminster and a recognition that it continued to wield real power in the realm of political patronage kept these ambitious young politicians nominally faithful for a time. The prospect of the end of Tory hegemony also served as an important incentive for the growing number of Catholic students and graduates who sought to play a part in the political and intellectual life of their country. Through the YIB they endeavoured to reform the organisation from within by censoring any evidence of renewed party dependence on the Liberal Party and attempting to ensure that the Irish

Party did not fall into the faction-ridden quagmire it had clawed its way out of ten years after the split; it did not seem to occur to them that their own spirited attacks on the alleged conformism of the IPP might contribute to further factionalism. The YIB favoured a 'fighting policy', the development of a more open and democratic Irish Party and a commitment to genuine Home Rule as opposed to devolution. YIBs were particularly critical of the Liberal government: the maintenance of the party's independence from the Liberals was a cornerstone of YIB thinking. As Francis Sheehy Skeffington argued, the YIB was

> not satisfied to advocate Home Rule; we want to get it. We think that the way to get it is to go back to the old policy of independent opposition; to oppose strenuously in Ireland, in Parliament, and in the British constituencies, every British Government that refuses or postpones Home Rule. We are not Sinn Féiners; at least, not in the narrow political sense of desiring the Irish party to abstain from Westminster. But we don't want the Irish party to go there to accept responsibility for Land Bills and University Bills, and to agitate for numberless other minor reforms . . . In short, we are growing impatient with the Irish Party.[9]

They proclaimed the necessity of this independence even more stridently after 1906 as the Liberals appeared increasingly unwilling to offer Ireland Home Rule and suggested a wide-ranging policy of devolution instead. Kettle stated in response that the Irish people had 'renewed their claim, not for any devolutionary humbug or extended local government, but for a democratic and generous scheme of Home Rule'.[10] The Irish Council Bill of 1907 was greeted with contempt by the YIB; and the fact that Redmond did not immediately dismiss it out of hand confirmed their opinion that the party had become subservient to its Liberal master. The YIB could hardly resist the propaganda opportunity offered by the

Irish Council Bill, but their disapproval of the proposed legislation – though unusually strident – was hardly novel as it mirrored general grass-roots nationalist opinion. Nonetheless, the party leadership evidently felt so alarmed by the opposition the YIB threatened to express at the upcoming UIL Convention that Joe Devlin was dispatched on its eve to talk the rebels round.

Kettle spoke strongly against the Council Bill at the convention, urging firmer opposition to the bill, but the more pressing issue for him was the defection of several IPP supporters, most notably C. J. Dolan, to Sinn Féin. Kettle published a less than complimentary critique of Sinn Féin in response, provoking a public row with Griffith. Griffith, in turn, set the tone for much of the future criticism of Kettle by referring to his excessive drinking and alleged earlier defection from Sinn Féin.[11] Kettle was subsequently accused on multiple occasions of having abandoned Sinn Féin after a youthful flirtation; one critic even claimed that Kettle had been elected MP on the strength of the Sinn Féin vote.[12] The North Leitrim by-election which followed Dolan's resignation was reminiscent of the earlier South Mayo contest; once again, Kettle denounced Sinn Féin for threatening the electoral hegemony of the IPP, claiming that Griffith's organisation had 'forced the fight'.[13]

Some of the diversity to be found in the YIB was reflected in the periodicals and newspapers to which the various members contributed. Men like Clery, who had taken to the Gaelic revival with far more enthusiasm than Kettle, wrote for D. P. Moran's *Leader*. Although they did not always support Moran's rather eccentric agenda, Clery ('Chanel'), Dawson ('Avis') and Kennedy ('Kappa Mega') – all three ex-auditors of the L&H – used the *Leader* as a forum for the expression of their own often unconventional ideas.[14] Though he was enormously critical of the Irish Party and the YIB at times, Moran initially welcomed the formation of the YIB, hoping a new generation of Irishmen would revitalise nationalist politics.[15] Kettle, however, remained suspicious of Moran. Though he stated that the *Leader* had played an important role in industrial generation, and endorsed its dismissal of Sinn Féin's economic policy, he also condemned the paper's 'blindnesses and bludgeon-ings'.[16] Yet Kettle was one of the few who would remain faithful to the party in the years to come. In the context and aftermath of the Home Rule crisis, Ulster resistance and the Great War, many of his contemporaries were compelled to choose between the strains of nationalism which they had once attempted to reconcile. Though it is difficult in retrospect to see how Redmond and his party could have taken any route but the one which ensured their own unhappy destiny in the difficult years after 1911, it is important to recognise their failure to capture the support and imagination of the younger nationalists who had once been eager to join and reform the party. This was to cost the Irish Party dear after 1916.

The establishment of the YIB was initially welcomed by the party, which was no doubt delighted to be presented with a ready-made and eager allied organisation which had cost it no effort and little expense. The IPP at first allowed the organisation the use of the UIL's rooms in O'Connell Street, but the YIB was forced to move its meetings to venues including the Antient Concert Rooms and the Students' Social Club in Dawson Street after some of its criticisms of the Irish Parliamentary Party were deemed too extreme.[17]

The establishment of the YIB signalled the development of a 'new and more keenly critical outlook on national affairs' among the 'younger generation of educated Irishmen . . . So far as University College was concerned, the spirit of revolution was not yet above the horizon. But a definite and lasting discontent with ineffective political methods had manifested itself.'[18] The spirit of revolution might not yet have found converts at UCD, but the society opened its doors to people who preached republicanism. One notable

speaker was Bulmer Hobson, a prominent republican, whose declaration that he and members of the YIB 'agreed on about 9 points
out of 10' is a good indication of the unconventional nationalism
and open-mindedness espoused by some members of the YIB.[19]

Kettle's involvement in the YIB clearly captured the attention
of senior Irish Party members who were at this time generally very
slow to notice talented young politicians such as Francis Sheehy
Skeffington and Cruise O'Brien.[20] John Redmond wrote to Andrew
Kettle in late 1904, informing him that he had been in touch with
the Bishop of Kildare, John Dillon and other influential nationalists
and that they had agreed that Tom Kettle would make an ideal
candidate for North Kildare. 'It would', he wrote, 'be a great pleasure to me and indeed to all those who in one way or another have
been associated with you for so many years in Irish politics if your
son could see his way into parliament.'[21] Kettle did not take up the
offer, perhaps because he wished to be admitted to the Bar before
entering parliament, or possibly because he was put off by the
financial burden of a parliamentary career. It is more likely, however, that Kettle was too preoccupied with other interests and
causes to contemplate entering parliament. He was a young man of
23, and it seems that he was not yet convinced that he could find a
place in an ageing party which seemed to be making little effort to
modernise and appeal to young voters. It was through the YIB
and occasional journalism that he was best able to broadcast his
developing political ideas.

Kettle delivered his presidential address before the YIB in
December 1905. Entitled 'The Philosophy of Politics', it was the
most lucid and comprehensive exposition of his political views to
date. He offered both a philosophical discussion of concepts and
institutions such as politics, ethics, and the state, and practical
examples of the uses and abuses of such abstractions both in Ireland
and in wider Europe. The speech was, in essence, an affirmation of

democracy and nationality, which for Kettle were the two funda-
mental components of the development of modern government
and sovereignty. He argued that, in common with other European
countries like Belgium, Italy and Germany, Ireland had been
affected by the transformation of such principles into political
reality during the nineteenth century and had similarly been shaped
by liberalism, democracy and nationalism. Thus, 'whatever gloomy
mood we fall into in the struggle for autonomy we have certainly
no justification for feeling lonely'.[22] True, he argued, these ideas
had also influenced nineteenth-century Britain, but Ireland's
history linked its political development far more closely to the
continent than to the British mainland. This strain of thought had
three main purposes: it highlighted political rather than cultural
differences between Ireland and Britain; it strengthened Ireland's
claim to nationhood by placing it in a context of successful
nationalist struggle; and it legitimised the Irish Party's dedication
to constitutional change and commitment to reasoned debate
rather than violent political struggle.

This kind of political discourse was almost unique in modern
Ireland. While James Joyce believed that Kettle's passionate ('too
demonstrative') engagement with the national question undermined his cosmopolitan credentials,[23] and a number of critics
questioned Kettle's claim that Irish identity and Europeanism
were compatible, others were enthused by Kettle's ideas. Although
extravagant, Clery's declaration that 'seldom has such a pronounce-
ment containing so much political philosophy, so many abstract
ideas been read before a branch of a working political organisation
in any country' conveys some of the novelty of Kettle's address.[24]
His rather Whiggish notion of the gradual spread of democratic
government and principles clearly implied a continuing allegiance
to parliamentary methods (he claimed, for example, that the
evolution of Irish democracy led to the abolition of tithes, Catholic

Emancipation and the Local Government Act of 1898), but it did not fit easily into the constitutional canon or the separatist school of thought. Kettle was, at this time, clearly borrowing from a range of influences and was enthused by contemporary political developments in Ireland. While he did not endorse the political programmes set out by Moran and Griffith, he did argue for a broader view of politics which would bring a range of cultural and political organisations into one liberal and inclusive movement whose central aim was Home Rule, not as a final solution to *the* Irish Question, but Home Rule as a first and essential stage in the democratisation and Europeanisation of Ireland. He was the most cogent and influential proponent of a new kind of constitutional nationalism, a nationalism that relied upon constitutional methods, but which incorporated modern strains of thought – both Irish and European – into its programme. Crucially and characteristically, however, he urged his young audience to acknowledge the primacy of political activity: 'call yourself a non-political as loudly as you choose, you will never succeed in ignoring politics'.[25] This was the rationale he advanced in the *Nationist*, 'a weekly review of Irish thought and affairs', when he founded it in 1905.

Mary Kettle claimed that the YIB and the *Nationist* were 'stepping-stones' in her husband's political career.[26] The YIB appeared to be having some impact on the Irish Party leadership, but both it and the foundation of the *Nationist* were daring endeavours for a young man who hoped for a political career. His support for the IPP was unquestionable, but his advocacy of constitutional nationalism was liberally tinged with suggestions for improvements within the party. After a few weeks of publication, Kettle invited Sheehy Skeffington to become assistant editor of the journal. He accepted, thus cementing the radical tone of the publication. Kettle's involvement with the periodical was short lived and exactly why his services as editor were dispensed with remains a matter for conjecture. William Dawson believed that it was most likely because the paper was not paying and because it was deemed to have adopted an anticlerical tone under his editorship. This was mainly due to Kettle's insistence that the IPP should be Irish first and Catholic after; the involvement of the notoriously outspoken and increasingly radical Sheehy Skeffington cannot have helped matters.[27]

Kettle and Sheehy Skeffington assembled a talented team of contributors including Curran, Kennedy and Padraic Colum. The *Nationist* served as an unofficial organ of the YIB: despite the disapproval of Redmond and other senior IPP members, the journal supported women's suffrage and sympathised with Dublin's poor. Both editors had, by 1905, accumulated a great deal of experience as journalists and their close involvement with *St Stephen's* had provided them with a good idea of the practical workings of a newspaper. Their decision to launch this new enterprise reflected their dissatisfaction with the agendas of other journals; it might also have been a direct challenge to the popularity of Moran's *Leader* to which so many of their friends had begun to contribute.[28] Through the *Nationist*, they were free to pursue their own favoured issues without editorial interference, and they could unveil their own political agenda.

In the first issue of the *Nationist*, Kettle outlined his policy and characteristically urged his readers to 'learn to accept Ireland as a great complex fact; an organism with all the complications of modern society'. He made this plea in the hope that the various national movements of Ireland would join together in the struggle for Home Rule. At the same time, he urged the party to remain vigorous and determined in its fight for Home Rule and to embrace some of the new ideas to be found in Irish political circles. He hoped to see an end to the divisions and distinctions between the language and political movements, but, as became quickly apparent, political progress was his major interest and aim. In a thinly veiled attack on the unreal expectations that some Irish-Irelanders attached to the ability of the cultural revival to rejuvenate 'national life', he denounced the tendency to regard politics as 'counting for nothing at all'.[29] The *Nationist* tackled a number of subjects, but its main concern under Kettle's editorship was the primacy of the constitutional agenda. This view was to underpin his political aspirations during the next five years.

CHAPTER 3

Parliamentarian and Professor

Kettle claimed that, while Parnell had a 'young party', Redmond's was 'middle-aged'.[1] Whether it was the activities of the Young Irish Branch and the sermonising of the *Leader* which finally convinced Redmond and the IPP elders that the time was ripe for the infusion of new blood into the party is open to debate, but in 1906 Kettle and his friend and fellow YIB member, Richard Hazleton, were finally and formally admitted into the party as sitting MPs. After being elected unopposed to a seat in North Galway, Hazleton played go-between, informing Kettle that Redmond hoped he would stand for the newly vacant seat of East Tyrone at the forthcoming by-election.[2] Kettle accepted the candidature, and after a tight campaign won the seat by a slim margin of eighteen votes. Redmond described the July victory as 'magnificent',[3] and the two young MPs were almost immediately dispatched to America on a successful though exhausting propaganda and fund-raising tour for the party.

Kettle's time in the USA was marred by quarrels between American constitutionalists and republicans. According to Arthur Clery, the bitterness expressed by the latter towards the party fixed Kettle 'in the constitutional view and made him ever afterwards very bitter against the extreme party'.[4] Kettle was unenthusiastic about the USA and clearly missed the cut and thrust of Irish politics. From New York he begged Curran to post him several books including two by Lady Gregory, *The Saxon and the Celt* by J. M. Robertson, the latest edition of the Department of Agriculture and Technical Instruction's *Ireland, Agricultural and Industrial*, de Jubainville's *The Irish Mythological Cycle and Celtic Mythology*, and 'any other information with regard to the present situation in Ireland, either in life or literature that suggests itself to you'.[5] Kettle's letters to friends and family, infrequent though they were, almost always contained information about what he had recently read or written or plans for further reading and composition. Requests for news from home also remained mainstays of his communications, his eagerness to keep up with Irish news when abroad never diminishing.

The serious business of parliamentary and constituency politics began in early 1907. Kettle spoke on a number of issues in parliament, but perhaps his most important contributions were to debates on women's suffrage and the Irish University Question. Fittingly, Kettle's first comments in the House concerned the latter, which was once again in the news. The Liberal administration appeared more determined than its Tory predecessors to solve this recurrent problem, and the IPP appeared to be eager to deliver a popular policy to the Irish electorate. As secretary of the Catholic Graduates' and Undergraduates' Association, Kettle had submitted a memorandum to the Royal Commission on Trinity College in 1906, outlining in no uncertain terms his association's poor regard for the ancient institution and declaring that, while his organisation was debarred from declaring in favour of any one particular scheme, it believed that the establishment of a second college within the University of Dublin which would cater to Catholic students would be an acceptable solution to the seemingly intractable University Question.[6] Kettle's views may have been held by most of his UCD contemporaries, but he found that his party was deeply divided on the issue.[7] Moreover, he was more aware than most of the complex and deeply partisan nature of the question: becoming embroiled in it was a risky business.[8] He nonetheless felt deeply that a final settlement was possible and that the issue should be kept alive in parliament. Having dismissed the ability of a number of his parliamentary colleagues to take up the question, he conspired with his fellow YIB member, Con Curran, and concluded that:

> There remains myself. I am greatly hampered by my youth and general newness. As however one is abused and accused of vanity whatever one does I intend to do just as much as I know how to keep the thing alive. I have a question down for tomorrow which may or may not draw Birrell . . . Things being thus it is necessary for me to become an encyclopaedia of the question, *and I rely absolutely on you*. You have done more than any one other person to provoke the present situation, and we must both take ourselves with a very heavy seriousness. Therefore I want you to send me on loan for a fortnight everything you have relating to the situation and the whole question. Send them at once.[9]

His hopes for a solution in 1907 remained unfulfilled. When Chief Secretary Augustine Birrell finally introduced the Irish Universities Bill in March 1908, Kettle welcomed it, not as a perfect solution, but because he felt that 'any Bill was infinitely better than no Bill'.[10] Birrell's proposal – which allowed for the establishment of the National University of Ireland with constituent colleges in Cork, Dublin and Galway – had at last earned the broad support of most interested parties, most importantly the Catholic hierarchy. Kettle was better acquainted than most with the opinions of senior clerics and their responses to the bill; he was particularly close to Archbishop William Walsh of Dublin who sought out Kettle's views on the constitution of the new university. Kettle, who had spoken in parliament about the importance of allowing women equality within the new institution, was, according to his wife, instrumental in persuading the archbishop to agree that women should be elected to professorships and tutorships at the same salaries as men; his intervention was subsequently appreciated by the university's first female professors, Mary Hayden and Agnes O'Farrelly.

Kettle had met Hayden and O'Farrelly through their mutual membership of the Catholic Graduates' and Undergraduates' Association, and he held both women in high esteem. He had also come to know them through his various activities on behalf of a number of Irish women's causes and organisations. His connection with Irish feminists was no doubt encouraged by his friendship and eventual marriage in 1909 to Mary Sheehy, a well-known suffragette and fellow YIB. Like her more famous sister, Hanna, Mary Sheehy was educated at the Dominican Convent in Eccles Street, before taking a degree at the Royal University as a student of St Mary's University School in Merrion Square, at that time Dublin's most academically prestigious Catholic university college for women. They moved freely in political circles and were both to remain politically active in organisations including the Irish Women's Franchise League (IWFL), the YIB and the Women Graduates' Association. Like Kettle, Mary Sheehy boasted an impressive nationalist pedigree. Both she and her sister were to lose their husbands in 1916, and though their politics diverged – Mary Sheehy supported constitutional nationalism while her sister embraced socialism and republicanism, exemplified by their respective wearing of the poppy every November and the lily every Easter[11] – their common commitment to women's rights saw them campaign together on issues including the new constitution and the restrictions placed on women's access to employment throughout the conservative 1920s and 1930s.

The couple's courtship was a long and seemingly difficult one. Few letters between them survive, but those that do reveal a certain hesitancy on Kettle's part coupled with frequent bouts of indecision and despair. It seems that they had separated at least once and had come close to doing so on many more occasions. Mary Sheehy – 'Maureen' in the couple's correspondence – urged him in 1908 to 'never again speak of our separating'. This, she declared, was 'impossible'.[12] She was troubled by his frequent depressive episodes and urged him to seek medical help. J. B. Lyons has suggested that Kettle's indecisiveness may in part be explained by his inability to provide the couple with the kinds of accoutrements which were seen as *de rigueur* in middle-class Dublin circles. It is true that financial worries would plague Kettle for the rest of his life and that he was acutely aware of the need to provide for his family, but it was his melancholia and excessive drinking which cast the longest shadows over his professional and personal life. Mary Sheehy referred regularly in her letters to her fiancé to his gloomy disposition, asking, for example, 'Why do you dwell on the black possibilities of life'.[13] She urged him repeatedly to resist the temptation to give into depression when she sensed a darkening of his mood in his letters. 'I see', she wrote to him, 'that you are allowing the black mood to keep you company. You must not do that. Keep looking forward, always forward and that will help.'[14] Mary Sheehy hoped to work with her fiancé, being a budding writer herself, but there is little evidence to suggest that they accomplished this. In common with their courtship, their marriage was to be marred by ill health, the demands of political life and frequent separations.

The marriage finally took place on 8 September 1909 at St Kevin's Chapel in Dublin's Pro-Cathedral, presided over by Mary Sheehy's Uncle Eugene. The smart wedding breakfast was held at Belvedere Place, the presence of the Kettle and Sheehy families, Redmond, Dillon, Devlin and several members of the YIB leaving no doubt that this was very much an alliance of two of Ireland's most celebrated nationalist families. One observer described the wedding as 'full of suffrage atmosphere'; Mary Sheehy and several guests wore 'Votes for Women' badges, and women's suffrage was mentioned in several of the speeches.[15]

It would be unfair to attribute Kettle's support for women's suffrage solely to his relationship with Mary Sheehy. He was well known before his marriage as an ardent supporter of women's rights, a cause he characteristically defended as a liberal and democratic inevitability. Sheehy Skeffington had been Kettle's major male ally in his crusade for women's improved access to higher education and Irish political life. An active feminist group which included Hanna Sheehy Skeffington and Mary Hayden targeted UCD, demanding the right to enter the college on the same footing as men, and swamping the UCD Rector Delany and Royal University senators with petitions and requests demanding that women be admitted to the college. They won few concessions and continued to fight their campaign through *St Stephen's* and a number of other pressure groups. Kettle and Sheehy Skeffington were two of their few allies within the college, and both men were intimates of many prominent female campaigners. Sheehy Skeffington went so far as to resign from his position of UCD registrar in protest against Delany's refusal to make concessions to the women's demands.[16] Kettle signed a number of petitions urging Delany to admit women to lectures and improve facilities for women at UCD.[17] In 1906 he delivered a lecture entitled 'Why Bully Women', linking the women's suffrage issue to wider questions of Home Rule and the democratisation of Ireland. Published as a pamphlet, the address urged nationalist Ireland (and offered a 'special appeal' to the Irish Party in particular) to accept that 'bringing freedom to the women of these countries' was essential if the British Isles were to aspire to genuine democracy. Women were, in his opinion, either 'citizens and should have the franchise, or they are voteless slaves and outlaws'.[18] Kettle extended his advocacy of women's rights beyond his student days and into his parliamentary life. In 1910 he declared that he 'would regard any Irish Parliament as an incomplete and a sham assembly unless the women of Ireland were represented in it',[19] and he spoke frequently about the issue in the House of Commons, becoming a well-known supporter of both English and Irish women's groups. Speaking in the Commons for the last time in 1910, he urged the Prime Minister, H. H. Asquith, to receive a women's delegation and attempted to act as something of a go-between between Redmond and suffragists. He supported the suffragette Emmeline Pankhurst when she visited Dublin and, sharing a platform with Mrs Pethick Lawrence at London's Scala Theatre in 1909, he used the propaganda opportunity at hand to link women's suffrage with Home Rule:

> He would remind them that the Irish nation found itself in a very similar position to that Union [the Women's Social and Political Union (WSPU)]. They were compelled to obey laws which they had no hand in making. But if Ireland was a nation deprived of liberty, womanhood disenfranchised was the greatest nation of the earth deprived of its liberty.[20]

Advocacy of women's rights led inevitably to further disagreement with prominent members of the IPP and, ultimately, to a deepening gulf between Kettle and some of his more radical young colleagues. Though William Redmond and a number of Irish Party MPs supported women's suffrage, John Redmond led a faction that manifestly did not; nor did he welcome Kettle's endorsement of the controversial issue. Kettle acknowledged that the party was split over the issue, but he argued that this divergence should not prevent it from being passed.[21] This sentiment appeared to be little more than wishful thinking as it became increasingly clear that the party was not going to endorse women's suffrage. This issue would return to haunt Kettle, even after he left parliament.

Kettle's election was of course seen as a great success for the YIB; he was the man who would bring the organisation's fighting policy to the heart of the party. Relations between Kettle and his one-time youthful conspirators remained cordial, but cracks began to appear as his new role as up-and-coming MP obliged him to side publicly with the party, even when its views were at odds with those of the YIB. His move into parliamentary politics also coincided with the radicalisation of the YIB, particularly under the influence of Cruise O'Brien and Francis Sheehy Skeffington, both of whom were increasingly critical of the IPP. While he was in London on parliamentary business, Mary Sheehy kept Kettle informed of the goings-on of the YIB and the L&H. She complained bitterly that the party had once again attempted to restrict the freedom of speech of the YIB and asked her fiancé to bring this to the attention of Redmond.[22] Denis Johnson, national secretary of the UIL, had refused to allow the YIB use of rooms for its next meeting at which Francis Sheehy Skeffington was to speak on Home Rule. Johnson no doubt wished to circumvent what was almost certainly going to be criticism of the party as the YIB had redoubled its calls for the IPP to assert its independence from the Liberals. Mary Sheehy asked her fiancé repeatedly to intervene on behalf of the YIB, explaining that the branch was to be 'suppressed because it has dared to think and express its thoughts fearlessly and openly'. She appeared to be exasperated by Kettle's failure to sway party opinion on the matter, asking him finally 'what side are you on?'[23] Sheehy Skeffington had also approached Kettle, hoping that his status as MP would persuade Redmond and Dillon in particular to allow the YIB a greater say in party procedure and policy. But, as Kettle told Sheehy Skeffington, 'it is no use'; the YIB was not going to be encouraged by the party.[24] Kettle's failure to, as Mary Sheehy put it, 'be on the fighting side' and to have Johnson's decision reversed surely contributed to his rapidly deteriorating relationship with the Sheehy Skeffingtons, whose politics were in any case heading in a radical direction of which Kettle did not approve.[25]

Youthful political allegiances were further stretched on more than one occasion in the following year. The turbulent National Convention of the UIL in February witnessed something of a showdown between an increasingly impatient YIB and the party hierarchy. The YIB proposed an audacious resolution to the convention, reinforcing its policy of 'concentrate on Home Rule – never mind the unessentials':

> That inasmuch as the establishment of an Irish Legislative Assembly in Dublin is the main object of the Irish Party in the British Parliament, and inasmuch as the English Liberal Premier has declared in the name of his Government that he will neither introduce a Home Rule Bill during this parliament nor undertake to make Home Rule an issue at the next general Election, we direct the Irish Party to accept no responsibility for any further minor measure, and to oppose and embarrass the British Government by every means in their power, in Ireland, in Parliament, and in the British constituencies.[26]

This was rejected at the convention, and after YIBs continued to offer IPP elders unsolicited advice, they were heckled and booed.[27] Opposition to party policy and disdain at the way the YIB had been, in the opinion of its membership, undermined and ridiculed at the convention further soured relations and undoubtedly placed Kettle – as YIB and MP – in an uncomfortable position.[28] To make matters worse, Kettle had agreed to sponsor a resolution for women's suffrage which had been suggested to the YIB by the IWFL at the same convention, but pulled out at the last minute. Francis Sheehy Skeffington had agreed to make the first resolution for the motion at the convention, and Kettle was to second it. The motion went ahead without Kettle, but the chasm between the young MP and the Sheehy Skeffingtons deepened as a result, especially as Kettle had allegedly backed off on the instructions of Redmond, who was reluctant to open the suffrage can of worms at the convention.[29] Sheehy Skeffington subsequently argued bitterly that 'every time the woman's suffrage movement in Ireland has relied on Mr Kettle at a crisis, he has betrayed it'.[30]

Kettle knew well that if the YIB continued down its belligerent path the party hierarchy would continue to attempt to silence it. Though Redmond had supported the parliamentary ambitions of Kettle, Hazelton and E. J. Kelly, he was not likely to endorse further factionalisation of his party and was positively determined to stamp out discord, especially when it threatened to spill into the public domain. His primary concern after 1907 was to preserve unity, not surprisingly given the splits and public rows which had beset the IPP since the fall of Parnell.[31] While endorsing a rigorous and independent policy for the party, Kettle too was ever concerned about the potential for the party to fracture into still more factions, and this was bound to bring him into disagreement with other members of the YIB. The next public disagreement came in May when, at a fiery YIB meeting, Kettle opposed a resolution which called on the Irish Party to break its present relations with the Liberal Party and to 'inaugurate a policy which would make government impossible in Ireland'.[32] Francis Sheehy Skeffington insisted that it was Kettle's 'duty' to inaugurate such a policy, but Kettle succeeded in having the second clause withdrawn.[33]

Hanna and Francis Sheehy Skeffington, in particular, had become increasingly wary of Kettle, believing that he had abandoned his attempts to reform and modernise the party and had become little more than a party hack instead. With Cruise O'Brien, they had also become outspoken critics of the Ancient Order of

Hibernians, an organisation that Kettle had joined. Kettle's respect for and abiding friendship with Joe Devlin surely increased their suspicions, especially after YIB delegates were removed from the Dublin City Executive of the UIL after Cruise O'Brien published an article critical of Devlin.[34] The fact that party leaders continued to refuse to allow women to join the IPP only strengthened their antipathy. Even the YIB, denounced by Hanna Sheehy Skeffington as the 'Young Men's Branch' of the UIL,[35] began to prove too timid for them.

Given that Kettle was one of Ireland's most vocal supporters of women's suffrage, the fact that he was to fall out most spectacularly with the Sheehy Skeffingtons and part of the Irish women's movement over this very issue in 1912 was deeply unfortunate. Tension between the IWFL and the IPP had grown as Redmond continued to refuse to make an open statement on his stand on women's suffrage and suffragettes and their supporters were increasingly roughly treated by stewards at various nationalist meetings. Hanna Sheehy Skeffington retaliated by resigning from the YIB and calling on her fellow feminists to follow suit. This caused dissension in the ranks of the YIB and the IWFL as many believed that Home Rule, so tantalisingly close in 1912, should take precedence over potentially disruptive and divisive feminist protests against the party.[36]

Kettle went further than most, resigning his (associate) membership of the IWFL. As sincerely as he felt about women's suffrage, he believed he had no choice as the IWFL had

> declared war on the Irish Party. To me the Irish Party remains the indispensable instrument of the political redemption of Ireland. Anything that weakens it at this moment must inevitably cloud the prospects of Home Rule. It is, therefore, plainly impossible for me to associate with a programme of war against the Party.[37]

At the same time, he declared his intention of continuing to support women's suffrage and reiterated his pledge to propose to the convention that the local government register be substituted for the parliamentary register in the election of the Irish House of Commons.[38] Kettle understood the implications of his actions. Calling in to see his sister-in-law before the convention and not finding her at the IWFL rooms, he left a note in which he stated 'Dear Hanna, I called to let you abuse me. I am of course going to move a motion, but also to make it clear that even if no amendment whatever to any clause can be carried I think that the Bill ought to be accepted.'[39] Kettle did not, however, introduce any such motion or proposal at the convention, appalling the Sheehy Skeffingtons, whose biographers have largely concurred with their view that Kettle 'broke his promise' to speak for women's suffrage at the convention.[40] It is, of course, impossible to know exactly what was promised, as positions shifted according to changing circumstances reflected in the fiery exchange of letters between Kettle and various members of the IWFL just days before the convention. Francis Sheehy Skeffington subsequently insisted that Kettle had made a 'verbal' promise to Hanna Sheehy Skeffington that while 'he would not move an amendment, he would make a strong plea for woman's suffrage in the course of his speech'.[41] We cannot be sure about private pledges, but we can be sure that Kettle did make it abundantly clear that he would neither support nor propose any motion in favour of women's suffrage unless the IWFL abandoned its plans to provoke 'disorder in the streets' and to send hostile delegates to the convention.[42] Neither would he do anything which would compromise the Home Rule Bill.

The IWFL accused Kettle of bad faith; he in turn accused the league of becoming a mere appendage to the larger English movement. It was not political co-operation between the two groups which he opposed, but the violent tactics which the Irish group had begun to emulate. A constitutionalist to the core, Kettle supported feminist protests so long as they remained within the bounds of the law; he denounced as undemocratic the Cat and Mouse Act introduced in 1913, but he urged women's leaders, including Hanna Sheehy Skeffington, to resist violent tactics. In common with many former supporters of the IWFL, Kettle believed that militancy would damage the women's cause, a belief that sat uneasily alongside his frequent and sympathetic descriptions of his father's own career as an imprisoned Land Leaguer and of the Land League in general, a militant organisation by any definition. Similar dilemmas would later present themselves with the aggressive tactics adopted by some striking Dublin workers in 1913 and with the rise of the Irish Volunteers.

Like all politicians, Kettle was forced to make concessions and compromises and was prudent enough to know that this was his fate. As he wrote about the International Socialists Congress held in 1907:

> If one never got tired, one would always be with the revolutionaries, the re-makers, with Fourier and Kropotkin. But the soul's energy is strictly limited; and with weariness there comes the need for compromise, for 'machines', for reputation and routine. Fatigue is the beginning of political wisdom.[43]

In 1912, he could not have been clearer about his priorities:

> As one who has been a supporter of the women suffrage before any of the Leagues began, and will remain a supporter of it after all the Leagues have committed suicide, I feel it my duty to say that for ' all Irish Nationalists, men and women, Home Rule comes first and everything else second . . . most of us will be compelled to remember that we are Home Rulers first and Woman Suffragists after.[44]

This was not merely the utterance of a party hack. Rather, it was a simple statement of the primacy of Home Rule, a primacy he had proclaimed since he first entered the political arena. Given his undoubted devotion to Home Rule and the widespread opinion that he would be likely to play a key role in the new Ireland, it appears strange that while the constitutional crisis unfolded and promised ever more for Irish nationalists, Kettle was actually contemplating his own withdrawal from Westminster. On the surface, his parliamentary career appeared to be flourishing: he had recontested and won his Tyrone seat in January 1910, increasing his majority and defeating his unionist opponent, the well-known son of Colonel Saunderson, no mean feat in a northern constituency. But, in the summer of that same year, he asked his East Tyrone electorate to release him as he could not promise to attend parliament regularly: his first duty was to the National University and parliamentary work had to come second. His constituents at first refused, and he attempted to combine his careers for a time, but he could not sustain this for very long. William Archer Redmond (John Redmond's eldest son) contested and won the seat for the IPP at the December general election. His friends and colleagues offered a number of explanations for his resignation: Clery believed that the discipline of the party was a strain for an idealist like Kettle, a view supported by Shane Leslie, who maintained that Kettle had been far too sensitive for the rough work of Westminster and that his genius had been unacknowledged by his fellow MPs. Kettle, he claimed, 'was too clever for the Irish party'.[45]

Another answer was suggested by his wife (who regretted that he had left politics): Kettle had been appointed to the Chair of National Economics at UCD in 1909 and he wished to devote himself entirely to his new profession. But this raises the broader question of why he decided on a career shift: this was especially mystifying in view of the possibilities presented by the looming constitutional crisis. He surely understood the potential criticism that would accompany his resignation: as he later wrote of Henry Grattan: 'A good politician and Parliament man, he was not: he committed the two deadly sins which are to sulk and to retire.'[46] Frequent crossings of the Irish Sea and adjusting to the customs of two institutions surely took their toll. It was also apparent that Kettle's political career was by no means unproblematic. Political squabbling of the kind he had urged the party to abandon dogged his own second election campaign in 1910. He had been warned by potential constituents as early as 1906 that he should curb his criticism of William O'Brien if he hoped to be elected in that year,[47] but the feud between the factions lingered on into 1910, resulting in public quarrels. In addition, it appears that he was forced to broker a deal between feuding Hibernians and Sinn Féiners in exchange for the latter's electoral support; this was essential if he was to keep the seat he held by such a slim majority. The crisis was averted and Kettle eventually increased his majority by 140 votes, but it seemed to point to a stormy period ahead.[48]

Financial hardship also played a large part in his decision. As he told the historian Alice Stopford Green, he had 'been getting poorer every month' he had been in politics. He found it difficult to live on his IPP stipend, and the new position promised security at £500 per annum. It is surely no coincidence that his marriage took place only one month before the UCD appointments were announced. Kettle also missed Dublin and his Dublin friends missed him, and his absences did little to fortify his relationship with his fiancée. Letters from Mary Sheehy feature numerous enquiries about the timing of his next trip home. Her attempts to organise a social life for the two of them was almost entirely dependent on his ability to get back to Dublin, and she clearly found the fact that his plans could change quickly most exasperating.[49] As 'his visits to Dublin were as those of angels and a great desire existed among those who knew him to enjoy as much of his company in the limited time available', he was often forced to squeeze visits into unorthodox parts of his busy days: on one occasion a group of young men accompanied him to the hairdresser's, where they continued their conversation with Kettle while the barber saw to his hair.[50]

Financial and social considerations aside, however, there is little indication that he enjoyed his time in parliament and life in London. Depression and drinking continued to take their toll on his health and happiness. He felt increasingly uncomfortable, even in the company of friends. In one of his more famous episodes, he had presided over a dinner at the Irish Club for Alice Stopford Green whose book, *The Making of Ireland and its Undoing*, had recently been banned by the Royal Dublin Society; he subsequently raised the proscription of the book in the House of Commons. He became a regular visitor to Green's London home, his wit attracting the famously gregarious historian. Very well connected herself, Green attempted to introduce Kettle to the capital's great and good, but her invitations were often refused by an increasingly tormented Kettle, who claimed that 'when I am done up as now, meeting new people is the more exquisite torture to me', no doubt a reference to his drinking problem.[51]

Mary Kettle claimed that her husband's parliamentary career was the 'happiest period of his public life',[52] and William Dawson tellingly claimed that 'divorce from parliamentary life was, for one of his temperament, nothing less than disaster'.[53] Two of Kettle's better known essays written during these years, 'On Crossing the Irish Sea' and 'On Saying Good-Bye', display a weariness with the constant travel between Dublin and London and a disillusionment with parliamentary politics. He was deeply interested in imperial and economic matters, but was frustrated by the lack of progress in these areas and the perennial parliamentary wrangling over

Home Rule. However, as his wife later claimed, his exit from parliament did not indicate a diminution of his political activities; it merely promised a new political arena, more freedom of expression and the possibility of the practical kind of work he relished.

He outlined some of his doubts about his prospects as a parliamentarian in a letter to Stopford Green, claiming that 'It is quite possible that I may not even be selected as Nationalist candidate – I have a lot of irritable and noisy priests. And if I am selected it is more than possible that I may lose at the poll.' He insisted that he would leave politics within the year as the current parliament was bound to be a short one, or within two years if the current session was longer than he expected.[54] The reference to 'noisy priests' is an intriguing one. By all accounts, Kettle remained a devout Catholic all his life. He was, however, an enemy of clerical interference in politics; such a view was consistent with his opposition to any outside organisation challenging the policy and electoral supremacy of the IPP, and was surely bolstered by his opposition to Healyite factionalism. Although he considered that the Church had a role to play in the dissemination of 'sane social policy',

> any attempt to formulate in the name of the Church a rigorous and exclusive social programme, and to insist that it is sound Catholic policy, must, of its nature, be futile and even dangerous. It is indeed part of the mission of the Church to safeguard these ethical truths which lie at the basis of all society; but when it comes to a discussion of the technical processes of society, economic and political, every man must effect his own synthesis of principle and technique, and he must be free to follow the light of his own conscience in his own experience.[55]

Nevertheless, a strong strain of liberal Catholicism permeated much of his published work, and his relations with a number of

prominent clerics remained more than cordial. Although Shane
Leslie believed that 'it was a miracle of intellect that he kept the
Catholic faith',[56] there is little evidence of anticlericalism in
Kettle's papers or speeches. He informed Redmond that he might
have continued to attempt to sustain two careers if his seat had
been uncontested or safe, but having to fight a further election
campaign for an insecure constituency while maintaining an
academic career would be expensive, untenable and unfair to his
constituents.[57]

Kettle's promise to Stopford Green that she would 'hear no
more of [him] in party politics, or sectional squabbles'[58] was either
disingenuous or remarkably naive. Not only did he continue to be
a vocal and well-known supporter of the party and Home Rule in
general, but he also kept up his involvement in a number of other
political causes including electoral reform as well, serving as a Vice-
President of the Proportional Representation Society of Ireland.[59]
Politics continued to overshadow his life: even his appointment to
the UCD professorship took on a decidedly political character.
The appointment had been viewed with suspicion from the outset
and had provoked a public controversy, which smacked of section-
alism. Far from distancing him from the party, Kettle's new academic
career appeared to many critics to be a perfect example of the kind
of jobbery and place-hunting which plagued the IPP and had long
been a target for its enemies. His good relations with Archbishop
Walsh and his long involvement with the university debate
certainly assisted his election to the chair, a position he had actively
sought. He utilised his religious and political connections in his
efforts to secure the post, obtaining, for example, a testimonial
from T. P. Gill, Secretary of the Department of Agriculture and
Technical Instruction, who made an exception for Kettle to his
rule that the department refused to issue testimonials.[60] Similar
support was proffered by the Redmondite Bishop Kelly of Ross –

himself greatly interested and well versed in Irish economics – who insisted that the man who filled the position should be a 'true patriot' and that 'for the sake of Ireland, as well as for your own sake, I wish you success in your application'.[61]

Francis Sheehy Skeffington – who was probably more critical of his brother-in-law than Kettle realised – claimed that Kettle had helped to get the Chair in Economics created for himself by virtue of his deep involvement in the drafting of the National University of Ireland legislation.[62] He also told their mutual friend, F. J. Byrne, that '[Kettle] has left parliament, handing over his seat in East Tyrone to young Redmond the Leader's son. He is now, characteristically, rather sorry he is out, and thinks the party ought to have offered him a safe seat!'[63] Clery presented a gloomier picture, arguing that although Kettle knew holding both positions would be an arduous task, he hoped the party would reject his resignation, allowing him to continue in both spheres. Kettle's career, he argued, was from that point 'simply a career of despair'.[64] This ungenerous assessment probably owes more to Clery's own disaffection with the Irish Party and his disappointment at Kettle's continuing loyalty to it than it does to the reality of the situation, but his was not the only cynical voice. *Sinn Féin*, one of the chief critics of his appointment, alleged that Kettle's 'political associates made him Professor of National Economics',[65] a view both maintained in the radical press for years to come and promoted by O'Brien and his supporters. The establishment of the position itself came under scrutiny; what after all was a Chair of *National* Economics if not a political post? The appointment of other well-known nationalists and Gaelic enthusiasts including Douglas Hyde, Eoin MacNeill and Mary Hayden to college posts did little to assuage the doubts of critics who asked: 'You have a Chair of National Economics in your college. Have you also a Chair of National Trigonometry or National Biology?'[66] Implicit in Kettle's characteristic reply was the notion that Ireland was a separate nation with special economic considerations of its own which required modern analysis. Moreover, he left no doubt that the professorship was in effect a chair in economic nationalism:

A National Mathematics is absurd; a National Biology is not quite so absurd, seeing that every country has its own peculiar flora and fauna. When you come to a National Economics the incongruity has wholly disappeared. Plainly you can constitute for each nation under that title a branch of Descriptive Economics. Plainly since one nation is at one stage, and another at another, and since the economy of each is, so to say, steeped and soaked in its temperament and history; your corpus of fact will in each case be strongly individual . . . I suggest to you that the doctrine of Nationalism in Economics goes far deeper than that.[67]

Kettle's genuine interest in economic matters – more precisely in political economy – must not be discounted when considering what drew him to the position. As his friend J. J. Horgan argued, Kettle's intellectual interest in Irish politics led invariably to a serious consideration of Irish economic conditions. As a parliamentarian, he had been acknowledged as an authority on Irish economic matters; he had served on the Public Accounts Committee and he co-authored the Old Age Pensions Act 1908, an act he broadly supported, but which he believed had not been fairly applied to Ireland. For Kettle, the line between economics and politics was in the Ireland of his day a very fine one. As Kettle, Griffith, Plunkett and Moran consistently argued, economic rejuvenation lay at the heart of what Griffith himself might have termed the resurrection of Ireland. And such considerations had a special appeal for Kettle, who advocated above all else pragmatism, realism and modernity in political and economic discourse. He rejected the extravagant and unscientific claims about Ireland's economic potential made by Griffith, calling instead for reasoned and scientific consideration of such issues. As he himself argued, 'my subject is either of practical use or it is of no use at all. If it is the function of erudition to stand apart from contemporary life it is the function of economics to stand close to contemporary life.'[68]

His appointment to the Chair ushered in a period of intense literary and academic productivity. *The Day's Burden* was published in 1910, and was followed in 1912 by *The Open Secret of Ireland*, both collections of essays. *The Day's Burden* was an eclectic mix of politics and literature that Francis Sheehy Skeffington rather grudgingly described as 'not bad, but marred by the usual Kettlesque d facts [*sic*]'.[69] The collection contained in many of its essays, most explicitly in its introduction, an affirmation of Kettle's continental perspective and its implications for Ireland. He foresaw the criticism that such strident cosmopolitanism would provoke, dedicating almost the entire introduction to a discussion of why Ireland must look beyond its own borders for intellectual and political solidarity and inspiration. Though long, it is worth quoting extensively as it was his most lucid exposition of his aspirations for a sovereign *and* European Ireland:

To anyone who, glancing at the foreign names which recur in these pages, asks with a sniff of contempt, 'What has all this got to do with Ireland?' I do not know what reply to make. Something like this, perhaps: Ireland, a small nation, is, none the less, large enough to contain all the complexities of the twentieth century. There is no ecstasy and no agony of the modern soul remote from her experience; there is none of all the difficulties which beset men, eager to build at last a wise and stable society that she has not encountered. In some of them she has even been the forerunner of the world. If this generation has, for its first task, the recovery of old Ireland, it has, for its second, the discovery of the new Europe. Ireland awaits her Goethe – but in Ireland he must not be a Pagan – who will one day arise to teach her that while a strong people has its own self for centre, it has the universe for circumference. All cultures belong to a nation that has once taken sure hold of its own culture. A national literature that seeks to found itself in isolation from the general life of humanity can only produce the pale and waxen growths of a plant isolated from the sunlight. In gaining her own soul Ireland will gain the whole world . . . My only programme for Ireland consists, in equal parts, of Home Rule and the Ten Commandments. My only counsel to Ireland is, that in order to become deeply Irish, she must become European.[70]

European parallels for the Irish situation were hardly unknown; Griffith had of course introduced his Hungarian comparison, but Kettle's was both less specific and more wide-ranging. Though Kettle, like Griffith, considered the policies of Friedrich List, believing that 'every nerve and fibre of [his] science quivers with nationalism', he placed him in a broader intellectual tradition than Griffith, considering his thought alongside the ideas of a number of continental thinkers including Roscher and Wagner.[71] On a superficial level, Kettle's analysis clearly reflects his own love of European literature, arts and philosophy. More important, however, is the ideological assumption that underpins his logic. Kettle in effect proposed a variety of separatism, not the kind championed by uncompromising republicans, but a political status for Ireland that clearly differentiated it from England. In common with many Irish–Irelanders, he hoped to see Irish political life made separate from Britain, but rather than looking to the distant Celtic past for inspiration, he looked to nineteenth-century developments in Europe for models. This was precisely the kind of rhetoric that was sure to arouse the disapproval of the Irish-Ireland contingent. 'Is it not enough', asked one irritated critic, 'to be Anglicised without being European?'[72]

His dedication to liberalism found expression in his writing on economic questions and was probably intended to contradict both the concerns of unionists about the Irish economy under Home Rule and the protectionist outlook of Griffith and his supporters. He asserted, for example, that a nation degraded nationalism when it chose to 'identify it with isolation or aggressiveness'.[73] The Chair of National Economics allowed him the opportunity to harness his nationalist views to economic considerations, and no doubt lent some credence to his rendition of the traditional nationalist narrative of the economic exploitation of Ireland under the Union among some sections of the Irish public.[74] The economic management of Ireland was, he maintained, central to its recognition as a nation; just as 'tariffism and militarism' were the 'apes' of nationalism, free trade in 'ideas and commodities' was the 'desired regime of those who have attained maturity'.[75] Obviously meant as a criticism of protectionist Tories, this article was primarily an attempt to introduce philosophical and political elements to economic debate. He despaired of those who insisted on reducing the Irish Question to an economic rather than a political question; this was no doubt another swipe at Conservatives, aimed at the politicians who had hoped to 'kill Home Rule with kindness'. What he described as the 'new politics' had, he argued, managed to combine nationalism and liberalism in both the economic and political spheres:

[The new politics] substitutes an organic for the old atomistic conception of economic life. And in establishing the nation as a principle or organisation it establishes it also as a basis of sacrifice, and therein provides the only basis of Protection that is not intellectually disreputable.[76]

Kettle also produced a large number of pamphlets at this time, many of them on economic questions. Most of his work was met by favourable reviews, though – unsurprisingly – *Sinn Féin* claimed that his study of Irish finance was 'of no special value'.[77] In particular, his pamphlet, *Home Rule Finance*, provoked the hostility of *Sinn Féin* for failing to make a strong enough stand against British economic mismanagement of Ireland and providing unionists with a propaganda gift.[78] Never credited as a serious economist, he was nonetheless remembered fondly by most of his students and colleagues. George O'Brien, one of his first pupils and a future Professor of Economics at UCD, described Kettle as 'a professor of things in general'.[79] Another student recalled that 'Tom Kettle did not pretend to be a profound student of economic theory . . . his class was so small that his lectures were really conversations in which he did not hesitate to express opinions on many subjects far outside the field of economics.'[80] On fine days he would hold his classes in St Stephen's Green, very close to where his portrait bust now stands. Not all his students were admirers, however. At least one claimed Kettle was so busy making speeches up and down the country that he neglected his professorial duties.[81] This kind of condemnation was increasingly heard as Kettle became more and more involved with the Volunteers and with recruitment to the British army.

Despite his earlier predication, if anything Kettle's political activities multiplied after he left Westminster as his resignation allowed him a new, welcome degree of political autonomy. His first priority remained campaigning for the Irish Party and for Home Rule, but he continued to display his occasional dissent from general party policy. He was, for example, a supporter of Horace Plunkett's co-operative movement, despite the reservations of some nationalists who were suspicious of Plunkett's alleged unionism. Kettle

called for peace between the party and the Irish Agricultural
Organisation Society (IAOS), arguing that Home Rule and co-
operation were 'comrade ideas'.[82] He rebutted the idea that nationalists were forced to choose between Dillon and T. W. Russell on
the one hand and Plunkett and his associates on the other, urging
them instead to recognise that the idea of both camps had 'sprung
from the common gospel of self direction'.[83] The *Irish Homestead*,
official organ of the IAOS, remembered him fondly after his death
in 1916, noting with gratitude his gift of hundreds of books on
economic matters to the co-operative library in Plunkett House.[84]
But by far his best-known political campaign outside the realm of
constitutional politics during this period was his involvement with
the Industrial Peace Committee – an organisation he helped to
establish and then chaired – in its efforts to negotiate a settlement
between employers and Dublin's striking workers in 1913.

Characteristically introducing Hegalian theory to his analysis
of the dispute, Kettle claimed impartiality in his approach: 'the
workers have talked wildly, and acted calmly; the employers have
talked calmly, and acted wildly'.[85] He also framed his scrutiny of
the crisis in economic and social terms, no doubt hoping that his
status as Professor of Economics would add weight to his conclu-
sions. Despite his attempt at impartiality, it was apparent that his
sympathies were with the striking workers, and this was borne
out by fellow members of the committee.[86] This no doubt led to
severe strain within the Kettle family as his father had hired non-
union labourers to work his farm at harvest time when – apparently
on instructions from Jim Larkin – his own workers had downed
tools in sympathy with the city's strikers. Larry Kettle, Dublin
Corporation's Electrical Engineer, was involved in a dispute with
the Amalgamated Society of Engineers, and though he was cleared
of attempting to obstruct the society, the Kettle name was sure to

raise a hiss at any public meeting attended by Larkin sympathisers; Larry Kettle experienced this at first hand when he subsequently represented the Volunteers at public meetings.

Kettle had long been appalled by and genuinely concerned with the living conditions of Dublin workers; according to Gogarty, he described to a shocked Housing Committee the conditions in which prostitutes lived, declaring 'it's your housing makes whores'. In 1913 he argued in a series of articles in the *Freeman's Journal* that such poverty and indifference 'bred Larkinism'; socialism was for him a symptom of material distress, not a cure for it. The Peace Committee itself was split over the issue with some members, particularly Captain Jack White, arguing that accommodation with the employers could not be found. He subsequently helped to form the Civic League, the forerunner of the Citizen Army. Kettle and White had already clashed at an L&H meeting over the latter's insistence that he would offer his services to Carson if Ulster unionists were suppressed by force. White was subjected to a typically cutting Kettle put-down in the presence of a number of prominent nationalists, including Dillon. But White was to have the last word. At the final meeting of the Peace Committee he proposed that Kettle was unfit to preside; White himself took the chair after Kettle stood down. This had been provoked by Kettle's 'spectacular' arrival at the meeting: late, dishevelled, bleeding and quite obviously drunk, he carried a bunch of carnations and a bag of oysters. He was increasingly in danger of becoming a laughing stock, his drinking provoking embarrassment and sympathy in friends, but causing serious damage to his reputation.[87]

Despairing of what he described as the increasing possibility of 'a very apocalypse of waste, impoverishment, and social dis-organisation', Kettle had identified the turmoil he witnessed in Dublin as a form of 'industrial war'.[88] He was tormented by the city's slide into near anarchy, claiming that Dubliners might soon find themselves 'plunged into a tempest of violence compared with which everything we have experienced will come to seem like a suave breeze in June'. His apocalyptic prediction would soon materialise on the battlefields of Europe and the streets of Dublin.

CHAPTER 4

Home Rule, Partition and War

Kettle has been accused by memorialists of naivety on a number of issues, but for a man who advocated pragmatism and realism in politics, his underestimation of the force of unionist opinion stands out as his major political blind spot. His pronouncements on Ulster unionism wavered between the simplistic and the aggressively dismissive. His most sustained assault was published in 1911, unambiguously entitled 'The Hallucination of "Ulster"'. According to Kettle, 'Ulster Unionism, in the leaders, is not as much a programme of ideas as a demand for domination. In the rank and file it is largely a phenomenon of hysteria'. He admitted that 'a democratic vote hostile to Home Rule' was a 'conundrum', but claimed that it was 'a conundrum of psychology rather than of politics'.[1] Much of this article focused on the alleged bigotry and unreasonableness of 'Orange Ulster', and paralleled the ill-informed and zealous unionist denunciations of Home Rule that were so despised by Kettle and his fellow nationalists. Kettle was clearly aware of the possibility that unionists might resist Home Rule with force, but argued that unionist riots and protests would end in mere 'gunpowder-smoke'. Moreover, he claimed that unionist capacity for armed conflict was overestimated; not only did they lack the protection of the law, but 'the military traditions of the Protestant North are not very alarming'. Home Rule, he believed, would be able to withstand Ulster's 'bluff' and Ulster's 'might'; if unionists persisted in resisting it, they would be faced down by the forces of law and order. Though he devoted most of the article to parodying Ulster unionism, he did examine more serious concerns such as fears that Home Rule would mean Rome Rule and that unionists would be overtaxed by a Home Rule government. Turning to nineteenth-century examples of pan-religious co-operation such as the League of North and South, he concluded that though that initiative had ultimately failed, 'the stream of democratic thought had been merely driven underground to reappear further on in the century'.[2] Believing that further links had been forged between Protestants and Catholics through the initiatives of such men as Michael Davitt and Joseph Devlin, he determined that a 'new "Ulster"' was 'breaking its shell'.[3]

Though noteworthy, his failure to appreciate the force of unionist resistance to Home Rule was by no means unique; like most of his Irish Party – and indeed Liberal – colleagues, he was convinced that unionism was little more than a cantankerous façade which would collapse under the combined weight of majority opinion, moderate coercion and reasoned argument. Like Redmond, his own friendship with a number of Protestants, some of them unionist, gave him a false sense of the pliability of the wider unionist community and of its British identity; it is no coincidence that he numbered few Ulster unionists among his acquaintances. Moreover, like so many of his colleagues, he failed to distinguish between Orange bigotry and reasoned objections to Home Rule, and simply underestimated the support for unionists within the Conservative Party and the wider British public. His policy of dropping the words 'Home Rule' in favour of phrases including 'national progress' and 'national movement' when addressing East Tyrone unionists during his election campaign suggests that he had some notion of just how obdurate anti-Home Rule sentiment could be,[4] but his public statements on unionism – especially of the

Ulster variety – showed no such subtlety. As he told the House of Commons: 'Ulster Unionism [is] not a Party; it [is] only an appetite.'[5] Many of his numerous snipes at unionists and unionism were typically witty, but he was not averse to employing incendiary rhetoric too. He told a meeting at Skibbereen, for example, that 'the imperial forces and the police force of the nation should be drawn aside and that Ireland should be left to fight it out with north-east Ulster'; surviving unionists should be 'shot' or 'hanged' or subjected to penal servitude.[6] In mid-1913, he argued that the government was obliged to enforce the same kind of punishment on north-east Ulster as had been imposed on the nationalists who in 1798 had been 'either hanged or shot down like dogs'.[7]

His rhetoric was clearly brutalised by the worsening Home Rule crisis and inflamed by the establishment of the Ulster Volunteer Force and the Curragh incident: at the height of the Ulster crisis he told his friends that he would 'fight and if necessary die' with the Volunteers if it came to civil war.[8] Outraged by the audacity of a 'small and insubordinate section' of Ulster, he argued that the government had a duty to put down any attempt to resist the Home Rule Bill.[9] But his ensuing support for the Irish Volunteers should not be seen as merely a response to these circumstances. He claimed that the object of the Volunteers was to defend the Home Rule Bill and the Irish parliament; violence was to be avoided if at all possible, but he argued that what he termed 'self-defence' must be available to nationalist Ireland. The establishment of the Volunteers was, he argued, a 'very simple instance of the law of action and reaction':

> The threats of the cavalry officers brought a long process to a sudden culmination. Men of active and realistic minds understood sharply where they were. When over the conduct of political affairs there is brandished openly what Mr Churchill has called the 'Bullies' Veto'; when those who are trained and paid to make such bullying impossible

go about to betray their duty, the prudent citizen has but one course. However peaceful his disposition, he will immediately hunt round for a gun. That is the rationale of the Irish Volunteers.[10]

One of main reasons for joining the organisation was also to ensure that constitutional nationalism was represented within its ranks. At the first meeting of the planning committee for the Volunteers held in November 1913, it was decided that The O'Rahilly would approach Kettle and Lorcan Sherlock in the hope that they could be persuaded to join the organisation. It was thought vital to include representatives from all the major nationalist organisations and Kettle and Sherlock, the Lord Mayor of Dublin, were well-known Redmondites. Kettle declined the invitation to come to a meeting because he was 'unwell'; his brother Larry consented to join. However, Kettle soon changed his mind and became a prominent supporter within weeks.[11] By February he was pronouncing: 'I am personally grateful to the founders of a scheme which restores to me my self respect as a citizen and enables me to perform one of my highest duties in person and efficiently and not, as now, through inadequate proxies.'[12]

According to F. X. Martin, Kettle modified his position when he realised that the organisation was attracting more support than he had envisaged; any threat to the IPP's dominance over nationalist politics had to be colonised. By April 1914 Kettle and Eoin MacNeill were drafting a permanent constitution for the organisation, and during the following month he travelled to London to discuss with Redmond the future government of the Volunteers.[13] Unsurprisingly, he denounced the provisional committee's refusal to accept Redmond's initial call for the modification of the organisation's governing body. He endorsed the right of the Irish Party to have a strong involvement in the Volunteers, but he despaired of the possibility that the movement might be split as a result of political squabbling, and remained suspicious of the advanced nationalist presence within the organisation.

In July 1914, Kettle witnessed events that changed European history and would claim his own life barely two years later. As he later stated, the squabbling of the Volunteers seemed to him like 'a great deal of theatrical humbug' in comparison with events in Belgium.[14] Sent to Belgium to buy weaponry for the Volunteers, he managed – for the price of £285 plus £8 – to procure rifles and to organise a boat and crew to bring them back to Ireland.[15] He attempted to secure the co-operation of the Belgian legation, telling Redmond that it seemed 'a pity' for the rifles to lie at Ostend and Antwerp where he was sure they were 'not wanted'.[16] He dealt, while on this mission, directly with both Redmond and Devlin, which suggests that he continued to enjoy the trust of the Irish Party hierarchy. Redmond was delighted with Kettle's success and insisted that the rifles only be delivered on his 'written order'.[17] But this mission ultimately ended in failure and 'bitter disappointment' to Kettle as the outbreak of war put an end to his plans to send the guns to Waterford.[18] The procured weapons were eventually detained and handed over by the IPP to the Belgian government.[19]

Buying guns soon paled in comparison with the impact on Kettle of the mayhem he witnessed in the streets of Brussels during the German invasion. He remained in Belgium as a correspondent for the *Daily News*, travelling widely through the country and gathering information and recording the reactions of Belgians for his columns. He discussed the urgency of the situation with the Belgian Prime Minister and King Albert. His initial reports were as vivid as they were unequivocal, and before Redmond had officially called on Volunteers to go to the aid of Belgium, Kettle had declared: 'It is impossible not to be with Belgium in the struggle. It is impossible any longer to be passive.'[20]

Initially, Kettle had little time for strategic and high political reasoning, focusing instead on the brutality and violence he witnessed. Like most IPP polemicists, he came to link the war with Home Rule and the connected idea of the rights of small nations. But it is crucial to understand that Kettle's early response to the war was articulated entirely within the context of his humanist Christian worldview, which placed Europe at the centre of an ongoing process of democracy and liberalisation. His support for the war was not merely a demonstration of his loyalty to Redmond. European circumstances took precedence over immediate Irish concerns, a reading of events which some advanced nationalists could neither understand nor condone. Kettle's analysis was also based on his own reading of German history and philosophy which identified Bismarck, Treitschke and Nietzsche as architects of 'the gospel of the devil'. His consideration of the impact of the crisis on Ireland *per se* was particular and uncommon, especially in the early months of the war. In essence he believed that Prussian militarism presented a threat to 'Europe and civilisation', and this jeopardised Ireland's position in that community of nations. Though he was clearly horrified by what he saw, the war actually offered an ideal framework for the development of many of his long-held assumptions about Ireland's place in Europe.

This is, perhaps, where Kettle's view came closest to Patrick Pearse's; both men identified opportunities for the strengthening of Irish nationalism in the Great War. This is hardly surprising, as both had ingested a literary and historical diet rich in militarism and martyrdom, and from 1914 the notion of redemptive blood sacrifice gained a new and powerful currency. Thus, while Pearse hoped that the spilt blood of Irish men would lead to an Irish Republic, Kettle could demand just before his death: 'In the name, and by the seal of the blood given in the last two years, I ask for

Colonial Home Rule for Ireland.'[21] This comparison should not, however, be overstretched; unlike Pearse, Kettle neither advocated nor glorified war, describing it as 'an insult to simple men'. As he wrote just before he died: 'unless you hate war, as such, you cannot really hate Prussia. If you admit war as an essential part of civilisation, then what you are hating is merely Prussian efficiency.' His condemnation of war remained staunch, while Pearse's fertile imagination seemed to be stimulated by war. More importantly, each had different ideas about the possible rewards for sacrifice; in his last letter to his wife, for example, Kettle wrote 'if the last sacrifice is ordained think that in the end I wiped out all the old stains'. These 'old stains' were personal, not political.[22]

Upon returning from Belgium, Kettle launched another critique of advanced nationalism, denouncing in particular its refusal to support Irish participation in the allied effort. He condemned the '"physical force" school of Irish nationalist thinking' as 'naive and Prussian', and reiterated his conviction that Ireland's struggle for political autonomy paralleled the Allied campaign against German aggression in Europe:

> If we take our stand against Prussia we have got to take our stand with England. No Man could condemn more strongly than myself the weary centuries of English blackguardism in Ireland. But the poisoners of Owen Roe O'Neill are dead, and the hangers of Emmet are dead. Even in our own time, and in the last ten years of it, a new world has come into existence. The England of 1914 is on the side of the Ten Commandments, and it does not reside in the spiritual tradition of Ireland to desert the 'Ten Commandments' in order to gratify a hatred of which the mainsprings have disappeared.[23]

The ensuing Volunteer split infuriated Kettle, who made his characteristic plea to nationalists of all hues to work together under the aegis of the party and for the good of Home Rule. He became convinced that a dangerous triad of the Gaelic League, Sinn Féin and the Gaelic Athletic Association (GAA) had initiated the split and led separatist opposition to the war. He argued that the latter had 'always been a fortress of anti-English feeling, and of that type of political mind which professes to see no difference between Cromwell's day and ours'.[24] Kettle attacked these organisations with undiluted venom, most violently in an article entitled 'Why Kill the Gaelic League?' which provoked a journalistic war of words. In that article and in several others, he bemoaned the 'desperate homesickness for a Split' displayed with a depressing regularity by Irish nationalists.[25] He insisted that the maintenance of a strong link between the Volunteers and the Irish Party was essential, not just because of his fear that extremists might hijack the Volunteers, but because he saw in the organisation the kernel of what might become a genuinely Irish army.

Following Redmond's famous Woodenbridge speech in September 1914, Kettle called for support for 'what is practically the first Home Rule cabinet, and the first Home Rule premier, and to make real and efficient the first Home Rule army'. He was especially enthusiastic about the separate existence of the Irish regiments as they were the 'living symbol of the truth that this war is Ireland's war, and that Ireland for the first time in the passage of long centuries sends out her sons fully accredited to fight for the sake of Ireland and for Ireland's cause'.[26] He believed that Ireland's participation in the war offered more than merely an opportunity for the country to prove its gallantry and European dedication to liberty; it offered the chance for nationalist Ireland to display some of the institutions of nationhood. As Alvin Jackson has argued, Redmond quite likely shared this aspiration, claiming that the establishment of the 10th (Irish) Division marked 'a turning point in the history the relations between Ireland and the Empire', and declaring that Ireland had for the first time 'put a national army in the field'.[27]

Both Redmond and Kettle wanted the National Volunteers to be recognised and hoped to win from the War Office a distinct Irish army corps, or at the very least divisional badges and recognition for the 16th Division. Desperately attempting to keep Home Rule and the future of Ireland after the war on the political agenda, their military aspirations reflected their dominionist leanings. Their hope that nationalist Ireland would form the nucleus of a quasi-national army on the model of Canada or Australia meshed perfectly with Kettle's insistence that the European war '[held] out to Ireland fair and high promise of the future'.[28] Kettle also understood the good sense in playing down the Britishness of the army, emphasising instead the distinct nationality, the common Europeanism and the free will of Irish soldiers. He suggested to Lord Kitchener, the British Secretary of State for War, that British military officers and their Union Jacks be shipped to Holyhead and that a French military band be allowed to march through Ireland, waving the tricolour and encouraging Irish men to join the French army if they so chose. Unsurprisingly, Kitchener found such a suggestion bizarre, prompting Kettle to threaten to enlist a corps of Irishmen in the ranks of the French or Belgian armies.[29]

Though critical of the War Office on occasion, Kettle was more concerned with the impact on recruitment of advanced nationalists. As he explained to General Hammond, Chief Staff Officer of the 16th (Irish) Division, in late 1914:

The first thing I noticed on coming back to Ireland was the absence of cheap literature on the right side. You have a daily, a weekly, and a monthly all chorusing the praises of Germany, and denying her barbarities in Belgium. Our decenter press, of course, explained at the beginning the justice of the cause of the Allies, *but they don't keep rubbing it in*. Now the problem in Ireland is to get at the individual conscience ... What has to be done is to put in the field a cheap counter-literature.[30]

His disapproval of these independents was a product of his gen-uine concern about their political activities and potential impact on recruitment figures, but also owed much to the distress created by their frequent attacks on his character. He was an obvious target for the underground press, which was particularly eager to condemn him for urging young Irish men to go into a battle which he himself avoided by appealing to the significance of his work as a recruiter.[31] In reality, however, he asserted from November 1914 that encouraging others to go to France and Flanders while he remained in Ireland was immoral.[32] Consequently, he attempted to enlist for active service on several occasions, but his health pre-vented his going. He did not, as some historians have suggested, volunteer for active service only as a response to the Easter Rising, or because he had become so disillusioned with the war by 1916 that he harboured a 'death-wish'. With his friend Stephen Gwynn, he became one of the best-known and hardest working recruiters, making, according to his wife, 'over two hundred speeches through-out Ireland'.[33] Gwynn described Kettle as 'the most brilliant speaker, taking all in all, that I have ever heard'. He also recognised from the outset that Kettle's support for the allied war effort was more complex than was usual:

> Kettle was always to some extent in revolt against the theories of the Gaelic League, which he thought tended to make Ireland insular morally as well as materially. He was a good European because he was a good Irishman; and because he was both, he was, though largely educated in Germany, a fierce partisan of France.[34]

Kettle announced his intention at the outset of the war to 'lecture anywhere in Ireland on the agony of Belgium, showing plates from photos'.[35] He was an obvious candidate for the job: he had witnessed events in Belgium, he was a well-respected writer on

European issues, and he was a gifted orator. Numerous references exist to his talent as a recruiter from 1914, and during his recruiting years Kettle also published widely on the duty of Irish men to enlist.

But the issue of his own enlistment – or lack of it – continued to haunt him as he published and lectured about the merits of the Allied cause. The details of Kettle's many attempts to enlist and his eventual success in securing an active commission are shadowy. He met with his first refusal on his return from Belgium in 1914; he was given the rank of lieutenant and assigned to recruitment duties instead.[36] This and a number of subsequent applications were rejected because of his 'ill health', a polite and imprecise allusion to his alcoholism. A sociable man who enjoyed company and conversation, Kettle's behaviour had at first been a source of amusement for his friends. But as he became an ever more regular patron of Dublin's bars and clubs, his excessive drinking became a cause for real concern. His personal papers contain few mentions of his condition, but acquaintances made references to it, usually by describing his poor health or absences from work. In 1913, Kettle himself addressed the problem, writing an anguished letter to his wife during what appeared to be a self-imposed period of exile in London:

> I do think that the miracle has been granted. Dublin as a focus of temptation has disappeared for me. When I come back – I wonder sometimes if I am to see you ever again – it will be to a return prepared in advance. The new life I mean to lead will be the life you suggest it was always my desire. With the exception of the one occasion of which you knew by intuition, or some strange transference of thought, I have not been mad. It is very hard for me to write anything at all. Somehow I got on to the fringe of shay Irish-London this time, and in every case of a fall from hope, decency and good repute I saw myself mirrored.

Take this as true – the old way is over. Whatever I bring back to you and Ireland it will not be the old sin . . .[37]

But the 'old sin', as Mary Kettle and their friends were soon to realise, reappeared in Dublin and continued to cast a heavy shadow over Tom Kettle's life. During the following year, he was sent to a private hospital in Kent to be treated for 'dipsomania'; he declared again that he had been 'cured' and claimed that he would return to a 'very different' world. His 'cure' was clearly temporary, as his alcoholism began to impinge more and more on his professional and personal life.

One of his most notorious wartime public appearances took place in November 1915 when he, Yeats and Pearse were scheduled to speak at a Thomas Davis Centenary Meeting at Trinity College. The event had been organised by the college's Gaelic Society, but ran into controversy after Trinity's Professor Mahaffy denounced Pearse for his anti-recruitment sentiments. The meeting eventually took place at the Antient Concert Rooms. Kettle appeared late and in uniform, 'gloriously drunk' according to Desmond Ryan, and was greeted with hisses, cheers and jibes about his condition.[38] Pearse expressed pity while Kettle displayed an embarrassing defiance as he allegedly banged the table with his fist and insisted on his right to free speech. The *Freeman's Journal* condemned the crowd for jeering at such a brilliant young man, but this embarrassing episode did little to convince either his friends or the military authorities that he was fit for active service. The life of a non-combatant soldier allowed plenty of time for socialising, and Kettle was frequently upbraided for appearing drunk in uniform. During a disciplinary meeting, he was told by General Sir Lawrence Parsons, commanding officer of Kettle's 16th Division, that his behaviour must improve: 'This cannot go on. If you don't obey orders, the British Army cannot hold us both.' Kettle's alleged response was 'we'll be sorry to lose you, General',[39] but his witty banter did little to disguise his deepening despair.

By early 1915 he was thoroughly disillusioned, and in an anguished letter offered his resignation on the grounds of physical unfitness: 'after many sleepless nights which have made a nervous wreck of me . . . there is no course possible except for me to ask leave to resign as physically unfit'. It is impossible to know what prompted this, but though he was under the ongoing care of Dr Cox, he was evidently in a very low state of mind and his alcoholism continued to take its toll. In what can only be described as a desperate letter, Kettle begged Hammond to accept his resignation with an 'expression of appreciation' so that his reputation and his position in UCD might be salvaged. Imploring Hammond 'from his heart' to arrange to have the gazetting of his resignation postponed for three months or a month, he explained that 'the moment it appears, a cloud of creditors will descend on me, and I want a little breathing space to escape something like disgrace'.[40] Kettle's reputation had been badly damaged by this time, with, on the one hand, advanced nationalists criticising his recruiting activities and his own failure to serve in the field, and on the other, his own friends, family and one-time admirers despairing of his slide into notoriety and despair. What is clear from all his surviving letters written in his small clear script during his final few years is that he longed more than anything else for a chance to redeem himself, to restore his shattered reputation and the 'chance to start really anew'.

He was saved in early 1915 from utter disgrace by the intervention of Hammond and another officer called Friend, who saved him from the 'racket of the Medical Board'. Kettle vowed to reform in exchange for a chance to make a fresh start. The jeers of 'the chattering gutter idealists' had increased after his ill-judged attempt to win the Irish Party's candidacy for an East Galway by-election in November 1915. Ever the loyal party man, he offered himself as a pledge-bound candidate, and his declarations to voters contained little more than references to the war; he told Colonel Hammond that he was standing on a 'support-the-allies programme'.[41] Kettle was evidently so sure that he would be given an active commission that he told potential voters that he would serve only an eleven-month term; thereafter, he would enlist. He failed to win the nomination, but this bizarre attempt to re-enter formal politics must be seen as an example of his determination to contribute to the war effort, albeit in a rather unusual and misguided way. Few friends and colleagues made reference to this embarrassing rejection, though the mosquito press lost no time in publicising it, most notably with a rhyme that began 'The Galway seat (who said defeat?)' and ended with 'Brave Tommy Atkins Kettle'.[42]

He evidently believed that he had reformed himself sufficiently to make yet another application for enlistment by the end of 1915. He hoped that his recruitment work would be repaid with an active commission and assured Parsons that he 'meant to get out to the war'; he insisted on 'no interpretership, staff post, or anything else provided I can carry through my training'.[43] He believed that he had received an assurance from Parsons that he could – 'by steady attention to back-door influences' – leave for the front with his division, but he required final clearance from Hammond. He implored Hammond to allow him to leave with 'any division', but though sympathetic, Hammond refused his request once again.[44] In late 1915 Kettle was in London, taking refuge from still more journalistic attacks on his character. Like many of his compatriots, he claimed that he wished to fight for a united Ireland under Home Rule, but what can only be described as his desperation to go to war must be understood in personal terms as well. He wrote time and time again about his desire to recover his 'honour' and to refute the accusation that he was a shirker. 'Will you', he begged Hammond in October 1915, 'take me back to any unit in which I shall be allowed to learn my work, to get physically fit, to do no recruiting, to take no leave, and to resume my honour?'[45] Active service appeared to offer the possibility of moral and physical recovery and, crucially, distance from 'the hotel and tavern life which brought [him] so close to damnation'.[46] His brother Larry told Hammond that Kettle's recruiting work had 'thrown him into the temptations he should have been kept out of' and insisted that 'Tom's one chance of putting himself right and starting a new page is to remain in the army *and go out to the front with his men.*'[47] Urging the transfer of his beloved brother to the front must have been a grim mission, reflecting both Tom Kettle's determination to go and his family's belief that it was his last chance of redemption. Hanna Sheehy Skeffington claimed that although his wife did not want to him to enlist, Kettle believed that he would have a better chance of getting over his alcoholism in the army, presumably away from the temptations of Dublin life.[48]

Accusations of cowardice and treachery multiplied after Kettle began to be associated with the pro-conscription camp. Deeply provocative though this seems, this stand should not be overstated. He advocated conscription only very rarely and it can hardly be described as a developed and resolute policy. In one of his few pronouncements on the issue, he stated in August 1915 that he had no objection to conscription if it would end the war.[49] In *An Open Letter to the Man on the Land in Ireland*, a pamphlet he published in 1915, which is sometimes described as pro-conscription, he made a special plea to farmers' sons who were widely believed to be shirking their responsibilities. Although he argued that it was the 'plain duty' of the Irish men (who could be spared) to fight, he also made clear that he would not 'impute unworthy motives' to the men who chose not to enlist. 'Every case is an individual case of conscience and for such there is no general rule.'[50]

To Kettle's bitter disappointment and embarrassment, after his requests to be sent on active duty were turned down General Hammond finally decided that it would be best for the army and for Kettle himself that he be 'invalided out of it'. He was sent away to recuperate and to wean himself off alcohol; there he faced a strict diet of regular meals and strong coffee to 'get over the worst times'. He described his affairs as 'pretty desperate' and castigated himself for betraying his ideals and his friends. His return to Ireland in early 1916 was a private affair; he remained remote at St Margaret's, avoiding Dublin's drinking establishments which had brought him 'close to utter despair'.[51] He once again claimed to be cured – 'the dominion of drink has fallen off me like an enchantment' – and begged to be given another chance, arguing that change was possible. Kettle's drinking had been compounded by his accumulation of debts; his UCD salary had been cut as a result of his commission, but his army pay could not make up the shortfall and there had been some confusion about whether or not he should be paid while on 'sick-leave'. He was beset by creditors, and liabilities which had 'reached the brink of legal proceedings'.[52] Finally, Kettle was saved once again by Larry, who promised to clear up his brother's financial matters,[53] and the intervention of Hammond, who arranged that he would in fact be given another chance, and sent on active duty with the 16th (Irish) Division's 9th Royal Dublin Fusiliers. Kettle thanked Hammond for helping him to 'get back, and be a man and myself',[54] and assured him once again that his drinking days were over: 'I have got so clear of the vice that had me at the point of ruin that I do not understand how it all happened. At all events I have taken a total abstinence pledge, and have been keeping it.'[55]

It is difficult to imagine the anguish he experienced while he took long walks, drank strong coffee and contemplated his future as he waited to hear from Hammond. His marriage was evidently in crisis, his university career in tatters and he was estranged from family and friends. Notwithstanding the 'cures' he had taken, his health was by no means strong; according to Denis Gwynn, 'that he ever reached France, in view of his physical unfitness, had been a marvel to his friends'.[56] It is not surprising that some acquaintances later described a self-destructive streak; as his wife wrote, 'some . . . hinted that he died in France because he had not the heart to live in Ireland. Some even went so far as to suggest that he died in France because he knew he ought to have died in the GPO in Dublin.'[57] She rebutted the claim and there is nothing to suggest that Kettle admired or was in fact sympathetic to the 'sacrifice' of the Easter rebels. The Rising had broken out while he was stationed in barracks at Newbridge, County Kildare. He had spent Easter with his family and was as deeply shocked and horrified as most Dubliners when he heard about the outbreak. Robert Lynd claimed that Kettle had helped to suppress the rebellion, but there is no extant evidence for this. He condemned the rebels, arguing that they had 'spoiled it all, spoiled the dream of a free united Ireland in a free Europe'. Kettle later referred rather frivolously to the Easter Rising as the 'Sinn Féin nightmare' which 'upset [him] a little'. 'But if', he explained, 'you tickle the ear of a short tempered elephant with a pop gun, and he walks out on you that is a natural concatenation of events.'[58]

He was also highly critical of the government's harsh response to the Rising and appeared as a witness on behalf of Eoin MacNeill, who had been court-martialled for his involvement in the rebellion. MacNeill faced twelve charges, most relating to his work with the Volunteers. This intriguing episode is difficult to verify, but it seems that Kettle, Maurice Moore and James Creed Meredith – who had been involved in the Volunteer organisation for almost as long as MacNeill himself – offered to appear for MacNeill. Their offers were accepted, against the advice of a number of MacNeill's supporters who were suspicious of their allegiance to the Redmondite National Volunteers and Irish Parliamentary Party. Kettle appeared at the hearing in an officer's uniform of the Royal Dublin Fusiliers. His friendship with MacNeill had remained intact despite the split; both men were UCD colleagues and former Volunteer collaborators. Kettle appeared to be willing to back MacNeill to the point of perjury; a note in the file relating to the court martial stated that:

> Liet [*sic*] Kettle is outside. He is ready to say He never though [*sic*] McNeill [*sic*] connected with any revolutionary enterprise. Believes the others deceived him will say 'split' was caused by efforts himself & other Redmondites to capture volunteers, etc. He is willing to help McNeill [*sic*] all he can.[59]

Ready to help though he was, his confusing evidence and rough treatment at the hands of the prosecution did not improve MacNeill's case; MacNeill was found guilty of all charges.

This episode cannot have done much to improve Kettle's opinion of the government's competence. His anguish was compounded by the involvement in the dramatic events of Easter week of a number of his family members. Larry had been held at the Royal College of Surgeons by the Irish Citizen Army after his car had been commandeered at the outbreak of hostilities, and his brother-in-law and fellow YIB member, Lieutenant Eugene Sheehy, had helped to put down the Rising.[60] But most disturbing was the murder of his brother-in-law and former political colleague, Francis Sheehy Skeffington. One writer has suggested that Kettle, sickened by the news of Sheehy Skeffington's murder, offered to resign his commission.[61] This seems highly unlikely, but there is no doubt that Kettle was disturbed by the military's response to the Rising. Hanna Sheehy Skeffington told Rosamund Jacob, for example, that her brother-in-law had been distressed by the news and had been reluctant to meet her in his British uniform, considering it 'dirty'.[62]

The Sheehy Skeffingtons and Tom Kettle had come to stand at opposite ends of the nationalist spectrum and it is clear that Francis and Hanna Sheehy Skeffington considered Kettle a traitor to a number of causes, including Irish nationalism, anti-imperialism and women's suffrage. They were also no doubt dismayed by his alcoholism and by the damage it had brought to his wife and extended family.[63] Francis Sheehy Skeffington condemned 'Kettle's contemptible selling of himself' and endorsed the idea that 'a bullet at the front [would be] the best end for him'.[64] Not surprisingly, these words appeared in Sheehy Skeffington's diary; harsh and embittered, they would have contradicted his reputation as a pacifist and humanitarian had they been uttered in public.

Kettle left Ireland for the last time on 14 July 1916; he sailed for France believing that the Home Rule Bill would be implemented in post-war Europe. Mary Kettle told General Hammond that her husband had 'left in splendid form and said to tell you he would make good'.[65] Kettle proved to be a sociable and popular officer, but much of his time was spent in the composition of letters and political treaties. His final writings may be viewed as a desperate attempt to justify the war and Ireland's participation in it, or they may be seen as a continuation of the propaganda work in which he had been engaged for most of his political life. It was most likely a combination of the two. He collected the thoughts by which he wished to be remembered and with which he wished to be identified; this was an activity common to many soldiers who knew that returning from battle was far from assured, but the impulse was no doubt stronger in a literary man. His most sustained piece was his 'Political Testament', in which he reiterated his belief that German aggression must be stopped and explained why Ireland had a moral and political duty to fight. In his final work there was a more sustained analysis of the impact of the war on the Irish political situation. Ireland was, as he said, his centre of reference, but the defence of Europe remained for him a worthy ideal: 'until the objects for which the allies went into the war are achieved, it must go on, and we mean it to go on, regardless of any waste of life or substance'.[66] He expressed doubts about the commercialisation of the war, writing to Hammond that 'the tone of some of the English papers, and the attempt to transform this from a war of honour into a war for trade, are unholy things, and breakers of faith, for Irish comrades at any rate, did not die that new Birminghams might arise'.[67] He also insisted that an essay, which protested against this, be included in a collection of his war-related articles. This volume was published as *The Ways of War* in 1917.

The 'Political Testament' conveys better than any of his other war-related writing the magnitude of the war's impact on Kettle. It also suggests a lack of awareness of political reality, owing in part to his absence from rapidly changing events in Ireland, but also to his optimism about the ability of the war to shift stubborn positions. This is most clearly seen in his references to unionism and Anglo-Irish relations. He had claimed as early as 1911 that the parliamentary future of the Home Rule Bill was safe,[68] and he maintained his argument that – despite some shortcomings – it must be accepted because it would give Ireland 'real power, real responsibility, and a real chance of growth'.[69] The Ulster Party, he argued, would continue to be a force in Home Rule Ireland: 'Captain Craig will dictate terms to us not from the last ditch, but from a far more agreeable and powerful position, the Treasury Bench. And we undertake not to grumble, for these are the chances of freedom.'[70] Of course, the unionists wanted no part in his plans for a Home Rule Ireland, no matter how genuine his guarantees of toleration.

His final pronouncements on unionism betray an equally ill-judged optimism, composed as they were in August and September 1916: 'The superb work of the Ulster Division and the changed attitude of Sir Ed[ward] C[arson] fills me with cheerfulness. Does it not seem exactly as if the right thing happened at last, as if English Statesmanship had thrown down its cards, and left the two great Irish Parties to come to a settlement?'[71] Despite the extraordinary difficulty involved in reaching a Home Rule settlement and the constant nationalist disappointment in both the Liberals and the War Office during the war years, Kettle also insisted that a new Anglo-Irish relationship had been forged by common participation in the war. The England of 1914 was, he argued, changed utterly. The England that made the Boer War 'was dead'.[72] It would be all too easy to put such statements down to war-induced jingoism and a desperate search for reason in an otherwise irremediable situation. But, hopelessly misjudged though they seem to the modern reader, such pronouncements owe more to Kettle's broader view of the war than they do to his understanding of temporal Irish concerns. For Kettle, the sheer magnitude of the threat posed by Germany rendered older disputes mere squabbles. He did not enter the war with the expectation of resolving these conflicts, but he never seemed to doubt that common participation in a righteous cause would strip them of relevance.

Kettle found life in the trenches difficult and his frail health continued to suffer. But, apparently having stopped drinking, Kettle assured Hammond that his 'one disqualification' had disappeared and that 'the stress of things here must make a new soul in any man', and he wrote prolifically between July and his death in September. He made no secret of the fact that conditions at the Front were atrocious, describing the 'chalk, lime, condensed milk, diabolical torturings of the air with unimaginable noises, and blood', and regretting 'the waste – the science of waste and bloodshed'.[73] But though he admitted that he feared death, his final letters suggest a man who had at last found some small measure of serenity. As he wrote to his brother 'I am calm and happy, but I desperately want to live'.[74] To another friend he wrote: 'I myself am quite extra-ordinarily happy. If it should come my way to die I shall sleep well in the France I always loved, and shall know that I have done something towards bringing to birth the Ireland one has dreamed of.'[75]

In late August Kettle's battalion was sent north of the Somme where major battles were being fought for possession of a number of positions, including Ginchy and Guillemont. Ginchy in particular had witnessed fierce fighting and a number of attempted Allied assaults, as it was situated close to a German strongpoint. Kettle survived the 16th Division's offensive at Guillemont, but his division suffered heavy losses in fighting in early September. Kettle prepared for the next attack on Ginchy and the strong possibility of death by attending mass, taking communion and writing poignant letters to his wife and friends in which he begged forgiveness for past sins. In his final letter to his wife, written only days before his death, he wrote 'the long expected is now close at hand'. Although he remained deeply ashamed of the misery he had brought her, he seemed to have made peace with himself and his past, declaring 'God bless and keep you! If the last sacrifice is ordained think that in the end I wiped out all the old stains. Tell Betty her daddy was a soldier and died as one. My love, now at last clean will find a way to you.'[76] To his friends – among them Hazelton, Redmond, the Cruise O'Briens and the Sheehys – he declared: 'What little I have to forgive I forgive freely, and what I have to be forgiven will I hope be forgiven.'[77]

His frail health had once again broken down, and he felt himself to be too old and unfit to lead his men. He believed himself to be 'about the worst platoon officer in the Division' and hoped eventually to be offered a position that would allow him to use his language skills or literary training, but insisted that it should not be 'a safe one'.[78] He was eventually offered a position as base censor, but he elected to remain with his division for its offensive on

Ginchy and led 'B' company out of its trench at dawn on 9 September 1916. He was killed almost immediately by a bullet to his heart: it had passed through a gap in the steel waistcoat he wore. The capture of Ginchy was the only Allied success on the entire front that day. Kettle's body was apparently buried by the Welsh Guards, and the precise location of his grave remains unknown.[79]

Epilogue

All surviving Irishmen of Kettle's age and generation, and I should say
most of their seniors, know what this name and these figures indicate
[1880–1916]; but at least one generation has come into being to which
they are almost meaningless.[1]

Mary Kettle was inundated by letters of condolence, each of
which spoke of shared experiences and lost opportunities. Perhaps
the most moving was written by his batman, Private Robert
Bingham, who praised Kettle's courage in electing to remain with
his comrades despite staff instructions, and spoke of the high
regard in which he was held by his men: 'He was a brave officer and
was like a father to me as I am my-self an Orphan boy, at the age of
18.'[2] His old friend, Oliver St John Gogarty, wrote upon hearing of
Kettle's death: 'Poor Tom . . . When the news came of Tom's
death, there were eyelashes, and not only women's, that were wet
with tears.' Known for his acid tongue, Gogarty was said never to
have had a bad word for Kettle, an honour he otherwise bestowed
only on AE (George Russell) and, ironically, Arthur Griffith.[3]

Gogarty's grief was shared by many of Kettle's friends, but it
was a grief often tinged with regret and disappointment: some
eulogies suggested wasted potential rather than achieved objectives.
This was hardly surprising as Kettle was only 36 and seemed destined to achieve much more in his life, but it was also a reflection of

the fact that his death coincided with the unfolding of two major political shifts: increasing anti-war sentiment and the decline of Irish constitutional nationalism. Most descriptions of Kettle's last years differ dramatically from the glowing accounts of the bright young man who stood head and shoulders above his contemporaries; rather, they are often steeped in disapproval, pity and even embarrassment. A partial explanation for this may be found in the divergent political paths taken by some of his UCD friends, most notably Francis and Hanna Sheehy Skeffington and Arthur Clery. But it is due mainly to his increasingly obvious intemperance and the growing realisation that his was not to be the dazzling political future for which he had once seemed destined. True, a few glowing accounts of his wit and intelligence may be found; his celebrity and talent did not evaporate overnight. But it was his tragic death that prompted the final enthusiastic appraisals, and the work of his wife and a few loyal friends which preserved not only his memory, but the memory of the almost forgotten Ireland they had shared. The list of the many hundreds of people who contributed to the memorial fund established by his friends to remember the 'most brilliant intellect of the younger generation of Irishmen' reads like a 'who's who' of the final years of constitutional nationalism. Devlin, Redmond, Dillon and many other IPP men of course appeared, but they shared space with many celebrated names in the arts, education, the church and the law. This list reflects Kettle's exceptional appeal to his contempories: it also serves as an extraordinary register of the hierarchy of a fast fading world.[4]

Kettle's desperate appeals to Parsons and Hammond were kept by the latter, who in 1937 shared them with Gerald Griffin. Griffin quoted selectively from the letters, claiming that what he included would 'reveal the real Kettle as he was'. This was clearly wishful thinking; though final letters from the battlefield did display undoubted courage and perseverance, most of the rest of the collection revealed a broken man. As Griffin confided to Hammond, 'those passages that show poor Tom's limitations are a secret between you and me and God'.[5] Kettle is best remembered for his participation in the war, and it is in this context that his recent rehabilitation began. Chroniclers like Griffin kept his memory alive through references to the Irishmen who served in the Great War, and his final poem, written for his daughter Betty shortly before he died, is frequently included in collections of Great War poetry. In fact, sections of this poem were quoted by the Taoiseach, Bertie Ahern, on the dedication of a Peace Tower at Messines, a site chosen because of its close proximity to where the 36th (Ulster) and the 16th (Irish) Divisions fought side by side in 1917. While Kettle's descriptions of the war as one being fought for liberty and as an opportunity for nationalists to bury their differences with unionists were condemned as jingoistic and disingenuous in 1916, they are now being quoted by the Irish Republic's leadership in its endorsement of both collective cross-border mourning of Ireland's war dead and the Good Friday Agreement.[6]

The lines quoted by Ahern were: 'Died not for flag, nor King, nor Emperor/ But for a dream born in a herdsman's shed/ And for the secret scripture of the poor.'[7] The fact that the Office of Public Works refused to allow Kettle's portrait-bust to be unveiled until 1937 (when it was dedicated without an official ceremony) was due to the insistence of his family and friends that these same three lines be engraved on the plinth.[8] In post-war Ireland such sentiment was seen to be inappropriate and highly inflammatory; in the early twenty-first century it is seen as reconciliatory and progressive.

Kettle himself prophesied in 1916 that 'what we have said and done is to be remembered and is to rise up in judgement against us in the new Ireland that is coming'.[9] His own reputation was a casualty of the 'new Ireland' that, until recently, rejected Irish participation in the Great War and, perhaps more importantly, denied the validity of the ideas that underpinned it. Kettle did not achieve the greatness for which he once seemed destined, but his ideas about Ireland's relationship with Britain and with wider Europe now appear remarkably prescient. Contemporary Ireland has in many ways become the country that Kettle yearned for: politically independent from but not overly antagonistic towards Britain; European, prosperous and outward looking. Kettle could not have foreseen that civil war, partition and a second world war would precede this national transformation. He would surely have approved of it, but he could not have imagined the price that would have to be paid for it.

Notes

Introduction

1 William Dawson, 'Tom Kettle: the essayist', *Studies* 20 (1931), pp. 599–600.

2 William Dawson, 'Kettle memorabilia', T. M. Kettle Papers (hereafter TMKP), UCD, LA 34/10 (13).

Chapter 1: *Family Life and Early Influences*

1 Letter from A. J. Kettle to the editor, *Freeman's Journal*, 22 Apr. 1912.

2 L. J. Kettle (ed.), *The Material for Victory, being the Memoirs of Andrew J. Kettle* (Dublin, 1958), p. xi.

3 M. Kettle, 'Notes on Tom Kettle', 1964, UCD, LA 34/11 (1), pp. 1–2.

4 *Freeman's Journal*, 22 Apr. 1914.

5 L. J. Kettle, *The Material for Victory*, pp. xx, xvii and 63.

6 Mary Kettle, 'Memoir' in T. M. Kettle, *The Ways of War* (London, 1917), pp. 13–14.

7 Mary Kettle, 'Notes on Tom Kettle', TMKP, UCD, LA 34/11 (2).

8 A. E. Clery, 'Thomas Kettle' in *Dublin Essays* (Dublin, 1919), pp. 6–7.

9 Oliver St John Gogarty, 'Thomas M. Kettle: a talk by Oliver St John Gogarty', TMKP, UCD, LA 34/9 (1).

10 Ibid.

11 Clery, 'Thomas Kettle', pp. 6–7.

12 *Clongownian* VIII: 2 (June 1918), p. 148.

13 Gogarty, 'Thomas M. Kettle', TMKP, UCD, LA 34/9 (2).

14 J. B. Lyons, *The Enigma of Tom Kettle: Irish Patriot, Essayist, Poet and British Soldier* (Dublin, 1983), pp. 21–2.

15 F. Hackett, *The Green Lion: A Novel of Youth* (London, 1936), p. 303.

16 'Tom Kettle at Clongowes' typescript, TMKP, UCD, LA 34/7 (9).

17 J. J. Horgan, *Parnell to Pearse: Some Recollections and Reflections* (Dublin, 1948), p. 202.

18 Mary Kettle, 'Notes on Tom Kettle', TMKP, UCD, LA 34/11 (2), p. 2.

19 Hackett, *Green Lion*, p. 290.

20 'Kettle at Clongowes' typescript, TMKP, UCD, LA 34/7(9).

21 Clery, 'Thomas Kettle', p. 55.

22 L. Levenson, *With Wooden Sword: A Portrait of Francis Sheehy-Skeffington, Militant Pacifist* (Boston and Dublin, 1983), p. 20.

23 W. G. Fallon, Notes for a lecture on Tom Kettle, 1930 or 1932, NLI, Fallon Papers, MS 22598.

24 P. Little in J. N. Meenan (ed.), *Centenary History of the Literary and Historical Society of University College, Dublin, 1855–1955* (Tralee, 1957), p. 90.

25 William Dawson, 'Kettle memorabilia', TMKP, UCD, LA 34/10 (5).

26 C. P. Curran, *Under the Receding Wave* (Dublin, 1970), p. 142.

27 W. G. Fallon in Meenan (ed.), *Centenary History*, p. 96.

28 Mary Kettle, 'Memoir', p. 15.

29 R. Lynd, *If the Germans Conquered England and Other Essays* (London, 1917), p. 137.

30 T. M. Kettle, 'On saying good-bye', *The Day's Burden: Studies, Literary and Political and Miscellaneous Essays* (Dublin, 1937), p. 103. The 1937 edition contains a number of essays which did not appear in the original 1910 edition: *The Day's Burden* (London, 1910).

31 L. Kettle to T. M. Kettle, 6 May 1901, Curran Collection, UCD, L 78.

32 Mary Kettle, 'Memoir', p. 15.

33 T. M. Kettle to Janie ?, 10–18 July 1904, TMKP, UCD, LA 34/1.

34 William Dawson, 'Tom Kettle: the essayist', *Studies* 20 (1931), p. 602.

35 R. McHugh, 'Thomas Kettle and Francis Sheehy Skeffington', *University Review* I: 9 (1956), p. 8.

36 R. Ellmann, *James Joyce* ([1959], New York, 1983), p. 61.

37 Gogarty, 'Thomas M. Kettle', TMKP, UCD, LA 34/9 (9).

38 Mrs Gogarty to T. M. Kettle, 20 Dec. 1903, Curran Collection, UCD, L 106.

39 Mrs Gogarty to T. M. Kettle, 1 Jan. 1903, Curran Collection, UCD, L 107.

40 Clery, *Dublin Essays*, p. 8.

41 T. M. Kettle to C. P. Curran, no date but most likely 1904, Curran Collection, UCD, L 68a.

42 Mary Kettle, 'Notes on Tom Kettle', TMKP, UCD, LA 34/11 (2), pp. 2–3.

43 Clery, 'Thomas Kettle', p. 3.

44 *St Stephen's*, vol. 1 (Mar. 1903), p. 233; Minutes of the Catholic Graduates' and Undergraduates' Association, Curran Collection, UCD; see also letter from Kettle and other students to the *Freeman's Journal*, 27 Oct. 1904.

45 *Hansard* (series 4), vol. 177, col. 892 (4 July 1907).

46 *Nationist*, 19 Nov. 1905.

47 Horgan, *Parnell to Pearse*, p. 202.

48 T. M. Kettle to C. P. Curran, 24 Oct. 1906, Curran Collection, UCD, CUR L 34/10.

49 See the 'Kettle Memorabilia' MS by William Dawson for more details on Kettle's time at the King's Inns and his tendency to indulge in practical jokes, TMKP, UCD, LA 34/10.

50 *Freeman's Journal*, 10 May 1899.

51 Curran, *Receding Wave*, p. 104.

52 For a discussion of Kettle's attitude towards Yeats, see: R. F. Foster, *W. B. Yeats: A Life*, vol. 1 (Oxford, 1997), pp. 298–9 and 358.

53 Ibid., pp. 280–1 and *United Irishman*, 15 Nov. 1902.

54 *Liverpool Daily Post*, 25 Feb. 1914; typescript proof, TMKP, UCD, LA 34/324 (2).

55 F. Sheehy Skeffington, 'Frederick Ryan', *Irish Review* 3 (May 1913), p. 117.

56 T. M. Kettle, 'The economics of nationalism', *The Day's Burden* (London, 1937), p. 133; originally published in the *Irish Ecclesiastical Record* 4 and 6 (1913).

57 T. M. Kettle, 'Would the Hungarian policy work?', *New Ireland Review* 22 (Feb. 1905), p. 321.

58 Curran, *Receding Wave*, pp. 145–6.

59 *Nationist*, 21 Sept. 1905, p. 5; T. M. Kettle, 'A note on Sinn Féin in Ireland', *North American Review*, vol. 187 (1908), p. 52.

60 Draft notes, n.d., TMKP, UCD, LA 34/289 (i).

61 T. M. Kettle, 'Would the Hungarian policy work?', pp. 322–3.

62 Gogarty, 'Thomas M. Kettle', TMKP, UCD, LA 34/9 (5).

63 B. Hobson, *Ireland: Yesterday and Tomorrow* (Tralee, 1968), pp. 9 and 23.

64 T. M. Kettle, 'Would the Hungarian policy work?', p. 325.

65 T. M. Kettle, 'A note on Sinn Féin', pp. 47, 49, 52 and 54.

66 T. M. Kettle, 'The economics of unionism': address to the National Liberal Club (London, 1912), TMKP, UCD, LA 34/139.

67 T. M. Kettle, *Irish Orators and Oratory* (London, 1915), pp. 402–21.

68 Clery, 'Thomas Kettle', pp. 2–3.

69 Minute Book of the North Dublin Executive of the UIL, Curran Collection, UCD, MS 24.

Chapter 2: *Political Apprenticeship*

1 J. B. Lyons, *The Enigma of Tom Kettle: Irish Patriot, Essayist, Poet and British Soldier, 1880–1916* (Dublin, 1983), pp. 132–7; see *The Times*, 24 Dec. 1912 for a general report on T. M. Kettle's views on ranching.

2 See, for example, T. M. Kettle, 'Reveries of assize' in *The Day's Burden: Studies, Literary and Political and Miscellaneous Essays* (Dublin, 1937).

3 T. M. Kettle quoted in E. Holt, *Protest in Arms: the Irish Troubles, 1916–1923* (London, 1960), p. 126.

4 Shane Leslie, *The Irish Issue in its American Aspect: A Contribution to the Settlement of Anglo-American Relations During and After the Great War* (London, 1918), p. 98. Mary Kettle believed that Leslie understood her husband better than some who had known him longer: Mary Kettle to Shane Leslie, 29 Nov. 1916, Shane Leslie Papers, NLI, MS 22829.

5 *Minute Book of the National Directory of the UIL*, NLI, MS 708.

6 F. Sheehy Skeffington, 'Frederick Ryan', *Irish Review* 3 (May 1913), p. 118.

7 William Dawson, 'Tom Kettle: the essayist', *Studies* 20 (1931), pp. 603–4.

8 Leslie, *Irish Issue*, pp. 97–8.

9 F. Sheehy Skeffington to the Editor, *New Age* (25 Feb. 1909), p. 371.

10 *The Times*, 23 Aug. 1906.

11 P. Maume, *The Long Gestation: Irish Nationalist Life, 1891–1918* (Dublin, 1999), p. 89.

12 C. O'Lochlain, 'Nationalist versus nationalist', *National Student* V: 1 (Nov. 1914), p. 11.

13 R. Davis, *Arthur Griffith and Non-Violent Sinn Féin* (Dublin, 1974), pp. 42–3.

14 P. Maume, *D. P. Moran* (Dundalk, 1995), p. 28.

15 *Leader*, 10 Dec. 1904.

16 *Nationist*, 21 Sept. 1905, p. 5; T. M. Kettle, 'A note on Sinn Féin in Ireland', *North American Review* 187 (1908), p. 49.

17 Fathers of the Society of Jesus, *A Page of Irish History: The Story of University College, Dublin, 1883–1909* (Dublin and Cork, 1930), pp. 491–2.

18 T. F. Bacon in J. N. Meenan (ed.), *Centenary History of the Literary and Historical Society of University College, Dublin, 1855–1955* (Tralee, 1957), p. 71.

19 B. Hobson to F. Sheehy Skeffington, 6 Mar. 1909, Sheehy Skeffington Papers, NLI, 21620 (i).

20 F. S. L. Lyons, 'Decline and fall of the nationalist party' in O. D. Edwards and F. Pyle (eds), *1916: The Easter Rising* (London, 1968), pp. 57–8.

21 Lyons, *The Enigma of Tom Kettle*, pp. 62–3.

22 T. M. Kettle, 'The philosophy of politics' in *The Day's Burden*, pp. 8–9.

23 R. Ellmann, *James Joyce* ([1959], New York, 1983), p. 63.

24 A. E. Clery, 'Thomas Kettle' in *Dublin Essays* (Dublin, 1919), pp. 9–10.

25 T. M. Kettle, 'The philosophy of politics', p. 2.

26 Mary Kettle, 'Memoir' in T. M. Kettle, *The Ways of War* (London, 1917), p. 18.

27 The irony was, as Dawson stated, that the next editor W. J. Ryan was a notorious anti cleric: William Dawson, 'Kettle memorabilia', TMKP, UCD, LA 34/10 (7–8).

28 I am grateful to Patrick Maume for this suggestion.

29 *Nationist*, 21 Sept. 1905, p. 4.

Chapter 3: *Parliamentarian and Professor*

1 T. M. Kettle, 'Mr John Redmond', *Liverpool Daily Post*, 25 Feb. 1914; typescript proof, TMKP, UCD, LA 34/300.

2 R. Hazeleton to T. M. Kettle, 20 June 1906, Curran Collection, UCD, CUR L 8s.

3 J. Redmond to T. M. Kettle, 28 July 1906, Curran Collection, UCD, CUR L 101.

4 A. E. Clery, 'Thomas Kettle' in *Dublin Essays* (Dublin, 1919), p. 9.

5 T. M. Kettle to C. P. Curran, 24 Oct. 1906, Curran Collection, UCD, L 73/a.

6 Memorandum submitted on the part of the Catholic Graduates' and Undergraduates' Association by Prof. W. Magennis and Thomas M. Kettle, Appendix to the First Report, Statements, and Returns furnished to the Commission in July and August 1906 (Universities and Colleges (Ireland): Trinity College, Dublin), [Cd. 3176], vol. 61, 1906.

7 T. M. Kettle to C. P. Curran, 23 Apr. 1907, Curran Collection, UCD, L 70.

8 For a full discussion of the Irish University Question see: S. Pašeta, 'The Catholic hierarchy and the Irish university question, 1880–1908', *History* 85 (2000) and S. Pašeta, 'Trinity College, Dublin, and the education of Irish Catholics, 1873–1908', *Studia Hibernica* 30 (1999).

9 T. M. Kettle to C. P. Curran, 23 Apr. 1907, Curran Collection, UCD, L 70.

10 *Hansard* (series 4), vol. 188, col. 826 (11 Apr. 1908).

11 A. Sheehy Skeffington, 'A coterie of lively suffragists,' in A. Sheehy Skeffington and A. MacLoughlainn, *Writers, Raconteurs and Notable Feminists*, (Dublin, 1993), p. 42.

12 Mary Sheehy to T. M. Kettle, 8 Nov. 1908, TMKP, UCD, LA 34/6 (7).

13 Mary Sheehy to T. M. Kettle, 28 Oct. 1908, TMKP, UCD, LA 34/6 (2).

14 Mary Sheehy to T. M. Kettle, 4 Nov. 1908, TMKP, UCD, LA 34/6 (5).

15 *Votes for Women* (17 Sept. 1909).

16 F. Sheehy Skeffington to W. Delany, 1904, Sheehy Skeffington Papers, NLI, MS 21641(I).

17 See, for example, Memorial to W. Delany, May 1904, Sheehy Skeffington Papers, NLI, Box V, Folder 17.

18 T. M. Kettle, *Why Bully Women?* (Dublin, 1906), p. 7.

19 *Votes For Women* (18 Mar. 1910), p. 387.

20 Ibid. (14 May 1909), p. 661.

21 *Hansard* (series 4), vol. 185, col. 259 (4 July 1908).

22 Mary Kettle to T. M. Kettle, 13 Nov. 1908, TMKP, UCD, LA 24/6 (13); 17 Nov. 1908, TMKP, UCD, LA 34/6 (17).

23 Mary Sheehy to T. M. Kettle, 17 Nov. 1908, TMKP, UCD, LA 34/6 (17).

24 T. M. Kettle to F. Sheehy Skeffington, 28 Apr. 1909, Sheehy Skeffington Papers, NLI, MS 21260 (ii).

25 Mary Sheehy to T. M. Kettle, 16 Nov. 1908, TMKP, UCD, LA 34/6 (16).

26 'The Government and Home Rule', typed pamphlet of instructions to nationalist delegates, no date, but almost certainly 1909, Sheehy Skeffington Papers, NLI, MS 22259.

27 Fathers of the Society of Jesus, *A Page of Irish History: The Story of University College, Dublin, 1883–1909* (Dublin and Cork, 1930), pp. 492–3.

28 See letter of F. Sheehy Skeffington to the *New Age* (25 Feb. 1909), p. 371, for a fascinating description of the quarrel between the YIB and the IPP.

29 F. Sheehy Skeffington, 'Redmond the fox', *Votes for Women* (10 May 1912), p. 508.

30 *Irish Citizen*, 3 August, 1912.

31 P. Bew, *John Redmond* (Dundalk, 1996), p. 28.

32 *Freeman's Journal*, 6 May 1908.

33 Ibid., and Lyons, *The Enigma of Tom Kettle*, p. 139.

34 F. Sheehy Skeffington to Molloy, 26 Mar. 1910, Sheehy Skeffington Papers, NLI, MS 21634.

35 H. Sheehy Skeffington, 'Women and the national movement', 1909, Sheehy Skeffington Papers, NLI, MS 22266.

36 See, for example, the letter of IWFL and YIB member, Isabella Richardson to the *Irish Times* (22 Apr. 1912) in which she protested against the IWFL's tactics as detrimental to Home Rule.

37 *Freeman's Journal*, 12 Apr. 1912.

38 Ibid.

39 T. M. Kettle to H. Sheehy Skeffington, 1912, Sheehy Skeffington Papers, NLI, MS 22663 (i).

40 See, for example, L. Levenson, *With Wooden Sword: A Portrait of Francis Sheehy Skeffington* (Boston and Dublin, 1983), p. 123, and M. Ward, *Hanna Sheehy Skeffington: A Life* (Cork, 1997), p. 78.

41 *Irish Citizen*, 3 Aug. 1912.

42 *Freeman's Journal*, 12 Apr. 1912.

43 T. M. Kettle, 'International socialists' in *The Day's Burden: Studies, Literary and Political and Miscellaneous Essays* (Dublin, 1937), p. 89.

44 *Freeman's Journal*, 19 Apr. 1912.

45 S. Leslie, *The Irish Issue in its American Aspect: A Contribution to the Settlement of Anglo-American Relations During and After the Great War* (London, 1918), pp. 95–6.

46 T. M. Kettle, introduction to *Irish Orators and Oratory* (London, 1915), p. xiii.

47 'East Tyrone Hibernian' to T. M. Kettle, 6 Sept. 1906, Curran Collection, UCD, CUR L 126.

48 R. Davis, *Arthur Griffith and Non-Violent Sinn Féin* (Dublin, 1974), p. 52.

49 Letters of Mary Sheehy to T. M. Kettle, 1908, TMKP, UCD, LA 34/6.

50 William Dawson, 'Kettle memorabilia', TMKP, UCD, LA 34/10 (14).

51 L. Ó Broin, *Protestant Nationalists in Revolutionary Ireland: The Stopford Connection* (Dublin, 1985), pp. 24 and 48–9.

52 M. Kettle, 'Memoir' in T. M. Kettle, *The Ways of War* (London, 1917), p. 24.

53 W. Dawson, 'Tom Kettle', *New Ireland* II (30 Sept. 1916), p. 340.

54 T. M. Kettle to A. Stopford Green, 28 Dec. 1909, Alice Stopford Green Papers, NLI, MS 15081 (8).

55 T. M. Kettle, 'Labour: war or peace' in *The Day's Burden*, p. 174.

56 Leslie, *The Irish Issue in its American Aspect*, p. 95.

57 *The Times*, 17 Nov. 1910.

58 T. M. Kettle to Alice Stopford Green, 28 Dec. 1909, Alice Stopford Green papers, NLI, MS 15081 (8).

59 Circular letter from the Proportional Representation Society of Ireland, 1912, Sheehy Skeffington Papers, NLI, MS 33611 (iii).

60 T. P. Gill to T. M. Kettle, 15 Aug. 1909, TMKP, UCD, LA 34/11 (i).

61 D. Kelly (Bishop of Ross) to T. M. Kettle, 27 Aug. 1909, TMKP, UCD, LA 34/211.

62 Lyons, *The Enigma of Tom Kettle*, p. 160.

63 F. Sheehy Skeffington to F. J. Byrne, 1911, Sheehy Skeffington Papers, NLI, MS 33612 (11).

64 Clery, 'Thomas Kettle', p. 11.

65 *Sinn Féin*, 9 Sept. 1911.

66 Lyons, *Enigma of Tom Kettle*, p. 197.

67 T. M. Kettle, 'The economics of nationalism', *The Day's Burden*, pp. 130–1; originally published in the *Irish Ecclesiastical Record* 4 and 6 (1913).

68 T. M. Kettle to A. Stopford Green, 28 Dec. 1909, Alice Stopford Green Papers, NLI, MS 15081 (8).

69 F. Sheehy Skeffington to F. J. Byrne, 1911, Sheehy Skeffington Papers, NLI, MS 33612 (11).

70 T. M. Kettle, Introduction to *The Day's Burden*, pp. xi–xii.

71 T. M. Kettle, 'The economics of nationalism', p. 138.

72 T. A. Fitzgerald, 'Is it not enough to be Anglicised without being European?', *Catholic Bulletin*, vol. 1 (1911), p. 84.

73 T. M. Kettle, 'The economics of nationalism', p. 134.

74 T. M. Kettle, 'The ravages of unionism (1)' and 'The ravages of unionism (2)' in *The Open Secret of Ireland* (London, 1912, repr. Dublin, 2007), pp. 52–61, 62–73.

75 T. M. Kettle, 'The economics of nationalism', pp. 134–5.

76 Ibid., p. 136.

77 *Sinn Féin*, 27 May, 1911.

78 Ibid., 9 Sept. 1911 and P. Maume, *The Long Gestation: Irish Nationalist Life, 1891–1918* (Dublin, 1999), p. 124.

79 J. Meenan, *George O'Brien: A Biographical Memoir* (Dublin, 1980), pp. 30–1.

80 Thomas Bodkin in J. N. Meenan (ed.), *Centenary History of the Literary and Historical Society of University College, Dublin, 1855–1955* (Tralee, 1957), pp. 134–5.

81 P. Nolan, 'Economics in the national university', *Catholic Bulletin* 10 (Feb. 1920), p. 91. I am grateful to Patrick Maume for this reference.

82 T. M. Kettle 'Sir Horace Plunkett: An appeal for peace', proofs, TMKP, UCD, LA 34/276.

83 T. M. Kettle, 'Sir H. Plunkett', newspaper article, n.d., TMKP, UCD, LA 34/276.

84 *Irish Homestead* 20 (June 1912), pp. 500–2 and 23 (Sept. 1916), p. 598.

85 T. M. Kettle, 'The agony of Dublin', *Irish Review* 3 (Nov. 1913), p. 446.

86 See, for example: T. Dillon, 'Early days in the new University College, Dublin', *University Review* 2 (1955), p. 29.

87 J. R. White, *Misfit: An Autobiography* (London, 1930), pp. 202–9 and 226–7.

88 T. M. Kettle, 'The agony of Dublin', p. 442.

Chapter 4: *Home Rule, Partition and War*

1   T. M. Kettle, 'The hallucination of "Ulster"' in *The Open Secret of Ireland* (London, 1912; repr. Dublin, 2007), pp. 74–5 and T. M. Kettle, 'The agony of Dublin', *Irish Review* 3 (Nov. 1913), pp. 98–9, 105 and 118–19.

2   T. M. Kettle, 'The hallucination of "Ulster"', p. 86.

3   Ibid., p. 87.

4   R. S. Sunderland, 'The life and times of Thomas Kettle' (unpublished PhD thesis, University of Dublin, 1980), p. 68.

5   *Hansard* (series 4), vol. 183, col. 809 (4 Feb. 1908), and Sunderland, 'The life and times of Thomas Kettle', p. 108.

6   P. Bew, *Ideology and the Irish Question: Ulster Unionism and Irish Nationalism, 1912–1916* (Oxford, 1994), pp. 72–3.

7   *The Times*, 2 June 1913.

8   William Dawson, 'Kettle memorabilia', TMKP, UCD, LA 34/10 (5).

9   *The Times*, 2 June 1913.

10   *The Daily News*, 2 Apr. 1914, TMKP, UCD, LA 34/282.

11   *National Volunteers: Constitution and Rules*, n. d.: Prof. T. M. Kettle named as a member of the National Committee and Laurence Kettle as one of Hon. Secs on the front cover.

12   T. M. Kettle, 'The Irish Volunteers: a necessary movement', *The Irish Volunteer* 1: 1 (7 Feb. 1914).

13   F. X. Martin, 'MacNeill and the foundation of the Irish Volunteers', in F. X. Martin and F. J. Byrne, *The Scholar Revolutionary: Eoin MacNeill, 1867–1945, and the Making of the New Ireland* (Shannon, 1973), pp. 147–8 and M. Tierney, *Eoin MacNeill: Scholar and Man of Action* (Oxford, 1980), pp. 130–1.

14   T. M. Kettle cited in J. B. Lyons, *The Enigma of Tom Kettle: Irish Patriot, Essayist, Poet and British Soldier, 1880–1916* (Dublin, 1983), p. 290.

15   Letter from T. M. Kettle, Belgium, 1914, Redmond Papers, NLI, MS 15199/6.

16   T. M. Kettle to J. E. Redmond, 13 Aug. 1913, Redmond Papers, NLI, MS 15199/6.

17   J. E. Redmond to T. M. Kettle, 25 Aug. 1914, TMKP, UCD, LA 34/135.

18   T. M. Kettle to J. E. Redmond, 13 Aug. 1914, Redmond Papers, NLI, MS 15199/6.

19   P. Maume, *The Long Gestation: Irish Nationalist Life, 1891–1918* (Dublin, 1999), p. 148.

20   *Daily News*, 8 Aug. 1914.

21   Mary Kettle, 'Memoir' in T. M. Kettle, *The Ways of War* (London, 1917), p. 10.

22 T. M. Kettle to Mary Kettle, 3 Sept. 1916, TMKP, UCD, LA 34/402.

23 T. M. Kettle, draft of an article about the threat posed to Ireland by the German military domination of Europe, *Liverpool Daily Post*, 25 Feb. 1914; typescript proof, TMKP, UCD, LA 34/394.

24 T. M. Kettle to Hammond, 1914. I am grateful to Kevin Myers for facilitating my use of these letters, and to Esther Murnane for allowing me to quote from them. When I consulted them, they were uncatalogued and in private hands, but have subsequently been deposited in the NLI. References to letters between Kettle, Hammond, Parsons and Griffin refer to this collection.

25 *National Volunteer*, 24 Oct. 1914; *Freeman's Journal*, 6 and 15 June and 19 Nov. 1914; see also T. M. Kettle to Hammond, n.d.

26 T. M. Kettle cited in Lyons, *The Enigma of Tom Kettle*, p. 269, and S. Gwynn and T. M. Kettle, *Battle Songs for the Irish Brigades* (Dublin, 1915), p. v.

27 Redmond cited in K. Jeffery, *Ireland and the Great War* (Cambridge, 2000), p. 41; A. Jackson, *Ireland, 1798–1998: Politics and War* (Oxford, 1999), pp. 197–200.

28 Gwynn and T. M. Kettle, *Battle Songs for the Irish Brigades*, p. vi.

29 W. G. Fallon, 'Notes for a lecture on Tom Kettle', 1930 or 1932, Fallon Papers, NLI, MS 22598.

30 T. M. Kettle to Hammond, 15 Nov. 1914.

31 See: *Eire: Ireland*, 23 and 30 Nov. 1914. I am indebted to Ben Novick for references from *Eire: Ireland*.

32 T. M. Kettle to Hammond, 15 Nov. 1914.

33 Mary Kettle, 'Memoir', p. 29.

34 S. Gwynn, *John Redmond's Last Years* (London, 1919), pp. 185–6.

35 T. M. Kettle to Hammond, 15 Nov. 1914.

36 There is only very sketchy information pertaining to his pension entitlement in Kettle's war file in the Public Record Office, London, WO 339/13445.

37 Sunderland, 'Life and times of Thomas Kettle', p. 260.

38 D. Ryan, *Remembering Sion: A Chronicle of Storm and Quiet* (London, 1934), pp. 164–5.

39 M. Dungan, *They Shall Not Grow Old: Irish Soldiers and the Great War* (Dublin, 1997), p. 121.

40 T. M. Kettle to Hammond, 13 Jan. 1915.

41 T. M. Kettle to Hammond, 15 Nov. 1914.

42 *Eire: Ireland*, 24 Nov. 1914.

43 T. M. Kettle to Parsons, 25 Oct. 1915.

44 T. M. Kettle to Hammond, 30 Oct. 1915.

45 Ibid.

46 T. M. Kettle to Hammond, 25 Mar. 1916.

47 L. J. Kettle to Hammond, 4 Apr. 1916.

48 Diary of Rosamund Jacob, 17 June 1916, NLI, MS 32582 (30).

49 Lyons, *The Enigma of Tom Kettle*, p. 278.

50 T. M. Kettle, *An Open Letter to the Man on the Land in Ireland* (Dublin, 1915), pp. 7–8.

51 T. M. Kettle to Hammond, 25 Mar. 1916.

52 T. M. Kettle to Hammond, 30 Mar. 1916.

53 L. J. Kettle to Hammond, 4 Apr. 1916.

54 T. M. Kettle to Hammond, n.d., but almost certainly 1916.

55 T. M. Kettle to Hammond, 24 Apr. 1916.

56 D. Gwynn, *The Life of John Redmond* (London, 1932), p. 525.

57 Mary Kettle, 'Memoir', p. 35.

58 T. M. Kettle to M. McLaughlin, 7 Aug. 1916, TMKP, UCD, LA 34/397(1).

59 Notes from Kettle, Meredith, Farrell and Curran for E. MacNeill's Defence, TMKP, UCD, LA/G/126 (16). See also, Tierney, *Eoin MacNeill*, pp. 228–9. The relevant file relating to evidence given at MacNeill's court martial is missing from the MacNeill Papers.

60 Sunderland, 'Life and times of Thomas Kettle', p. 308.

61 K. Tynan, *Years of the Shadow* (London, 1919), p. 81.

62 Diary of Rosamund Jacob, 14 May 1916, NLI, MS 32582 (29).

63 Lyons, *The Enigma of Tom Kettle*, p. 279.

64 F. Sheehy Skeffington diary entry, 29 June 1915, Sheehy Skeffington Papers, NLI, MS 22277; I am grateful to Ben Novick for drawing my attention to this reference.

65 Mary Kettle to Hammond, 17 July 1916.

66 T. M. Kettle, 'Trade or honour' in *The Ways of War*, p. 232.

67 T. M. Kettle to Hammond, 28 July 1916.

68 T. M. Kettle, *The Open Secret of Ireland*, p. 7.

69 Ibid.; MS notes concerning the Home Rule Bill, n.d., TMKP, UCD, LA 34/299.

70 T. M. Kettle, MS draft on the political problem to be solved in Ireland, n.d., TMKP, UCD, LA 34/289.

71 T. M. Kettle to H. McLaughlin, 7 Aug. 1916, TMKP, UCD, LA 34/397 (2).

72 T. M. Kettle, Political Testament, TMKP, UCD, LA 34/394 (1).

73 MS fragment of a letter from T. M. Kettle to 'J. J.', 1916, TMKP, UCD, LA 34/398.

74 Mary Kettle, 'Memoir', p. 35.

75   T. M. Kettle to H. McLaughlin, 7 Aug. 1916, TMKP, UCD, LA 34/397.

76   T. M. Kettle to Mary Kettle, 3 Sept. 1916, TMKP, UCD, LA 34/402.

77   T. M. Kettle to Mary Kettle, TMKP, UCD, LA 34/401.

78   T. M. Kettle to H. McLaughlin, July 1916, TMKP, UCD, LA 34/397.

79   Kettle's brother-in-law claimed to have located the grave in 1917: Eugene Sheehy to his mother, 18 Nov. 1917, TMKP, UCD, LA 34/93.

Epilogue

1   W. Dawson, 'Tom Kettle: the essayist', *Studies* 20 (1931), p. 598.

2   R. Bingham to M. Kettle, 27 Sept. 1916, *Liverpool Daily Post*, 25 Feb. 1914; typescript proof, TMKP, UCD, LA 34/4/4.

3   U. O'Connor, *Oliver St John Gogarty* (London, 1990), p. 177.

4   *Freeman's Journal*, 4 Nov. 1916 and 13 Jan. 1917.

5   G. Griffin to Hammond, 2 Feb. 1938; and G. Griffin, *The Wild Geese: Pen Portraits of Famous Irish Exiles* (London, 1938), pp. 141–6.

6   B. Ahern, Statement by the Taoiseach, 11 Nov. 1998; press releases and speeches. http://www.irlgov.ie/taoiseach/press/Archives/1998/10-11-98.htm.

7   Ibid.

8   It was only the extraordinary persistence of Mary Kettle, William Fallon and others that resulted in the unveiling of the bust. The long and often bitter story of the establishment of Kettle's memorial is outlined in William Fallon's Papers, held in the NLI.

9   T. M. Kettle, 'Why Ireland fought' in *The Ways of War* (London, 1917), pp. 71–2.

Select Bibliography

PRIMARY SOURCES:

Under-utilised by historians, Kettle's numerous articles, essays and reviews provide an invaluable introduction to his thought and to some of the political ideas circulating in turn of the century Ireland. His contributions to *St Stephen's* and the *Nationist* offer valuable insights into the early days of the YIB, as do contributions to the *Freeman's Journal* from 1904. *The Day's Burden* (1910) and *The Open Secret of Ireland* (1912) contain a number of indispensable essays on economic, philosophical and political questions, and *Why Bully Women?* (1910) is a good summary of his ideas about women's suffrage. 'Would the Hungarian policy work?' (*New Ireland Review*, 1905) and 'A note on Sinn Féin in Ireland' (*North American Review*, 1908) are two of his most interesting critiques of Sinn Féin and separatism. He published copiously during the war; some of his more interesting ideas were developed in the following publication: *An Open Letter to the Man on the Land in Ireland* (1916) and *The Ways of War* (1917), which has a useful though somewhat misleading introduction by Mary Kettle. References to a large number of his writings may be found in the footnotes.

SECONDARY SOURCES

J. B. Lyons's *The Enigma of Tom Kettle* (Dublin, 1983) is a fine biography which draws on a wide selection of Kettle's writings and papers. R. McHugh, 'Tom Kettle and Francis Sheehy-Skeffington' (*University Review*, 1956) and S. Leslie 'The killing of Kettle' in his *The Irish Issue in its American Aspect* (London, 1918) also contain much useful information. Kettle's death prompted a number of obituaries and reminiscences, the best being: A. E. Clery, 'Thomas Kettle'

(*Studies*, 1916) and W. Dawson, 'Tom Kettle: The essayist' (*Studies*, 1931). The following contain some insights into the Ireland of his day and his place in it: C. P. Curran, *Under the Receding Wave* (Dublin, 1970); J. N. Meenan, *Centenary History of the Literary and Historical Society, 1855–1955* (Tralee, 1957); J. J. Horgan, *Parnell to Pearse: Some Recollections and Reflections* (Dublin, 1948); P. Maume, *D. P. Moran* (Dundalk, 1995) and *The Long Gestation: Irish Nationalist Life, 1891–1918* (Dublin, 1999), and S. Pašeta, *Before the Revolution: Nationalism, Social Change and Ireland's Catholic Elite* (Cork, 1999).

INDEX